☞ Who Were the Founding Fathers?

WHO WERE THE

Founding Fathers?

Two Hundred Years of Reinventing American History

Steven H. Jaffe

HENRY HOLT AND COMPANY · NEW YORK

Henry Holt and Company, Inc.
Publishers since 1866
115 West 18th Street
New York, New York 10011
Henry Holt is a registered
trademark of Henry Holt and Company, Inc.
Copyright © 1996 by Steven H. Jaffe
All rights reserved.
Published in Canada by Fitzhenry & Whiteside Ltd.,
195 Allstate Parkway, Markham, Ontario L3R 4T8.

Library of Congress Cataloging-in-Publication Data
Jaffe, Steven.
Who were the founding fathers?: two hundred years of reinventing
American history / by Steven Jaffe.
p.   cm.
Includes bibliographical references and index.
1. United States—History—Revolution, 1775–1783—Historiography.
2. United States—Politics and government—1775–1783—Historiography.   I. Title.
E209.J29   1996   973.3'072—dc20   95-42581

ISBN 0-8050-3102-2
First Edition—1996

Printed in the United States of America on acid-free paper. ∞
10 9 8 7 6 5 4 3 2 1

In Memory of Two Parents,
Morris H. Jaffe and Terri Worth

☞ Contents

☞ Who Were the Founding Fathers?

Introduction
FIFTY-SIX TRAITORS

☞On the morning of July 4, 1776, fifty-six traitors stride into the Pennsylvania colony's statehouse in the city of Philadelphia. Some are fools, but most are shrewdly selfish and evil men. They are rebels against the king who has always protected them. For over a year, they have been in armed rebellion against the legal and just right of Parliament to tax them and to regulate their affairs. Their goal is to increase their personal power at the expense of the king's duly appointed officers. Today, they take their treachery even further. By the evening, they will, in a foul and daring act of treason, declare independence and thus announce to the world their intention of destroying the British Empire.

Or:

On the morning of July 4, 1776, fifty-six hypocrites straggle into the Pennsylvania statehouse. Most are wealthy men—landowners, lawyers, and businessmen—and all are white. The Declaration they will ratify this evening claims that "All men are created equal." But these statesmen will do little or nothing to challenge the great evil of slavery that curses their country. Indeed, most of the Southerners in the hall—including the author of the Declaration, Thomas Jefferson of Virginia—are there because the labor of their human property allows them to be. By proclaiming an equality that applies to white men only, these so-called heroes fail miserably, for they lack the courage to create what the world cries out for: a nation that lives up to its high-toned pronouncements on liberty by freeing its slaves.

Or:

On the morning of July 4, 1776, fifty-six patriots enter the building that will soon be known to the world as Independence Hall. They risk their lives, for they dare to challenge the most powerful empire in the world. They have spent the hot days of this summer debating the wisdom and justice of declaring the independence of the thirteen colonies united in resistance to British tyranny. Some doubt whether an independent American nation can succeed. Yet their dedication to the principle of government by and for the people gives them courage. By evening, they will have created the greatest nation the world has ever known, a nation committed to liberty, equality, and the rights of man.

Which version is the correct one? Each has been advanced as a true account by different people at different times. The British officials and American loyalists who embraced the first version, the radical abolitionists who believed in the second, and the nineteenth-century textbook writers who promoted the third disagreed about the true meaning of the events that took place in Philadelphia on the Fourth of July in 1776. And people have come up with many other interpretations as well. Over the past two hundred years, such disagreements have always shaped how Americans viewed their past.

This book is not a biography of the lives of the Founding Fathers. Nor is it a conventional history of the events of the American Revolution and the first years of the United States. Its aim is to show how people have interpreted and reinterpreted those lives and events. For two hundred years, Americans have been debating, disagreeing, arguing, and fighting over who the Founders were and what their lives meant. In newspapers and pamphlets, paintings and sculptures, novels and textbooks, ads and propaganda posters, plays, movies, and television shows, Americans have shaped and reshaped the identity of the Founders and the meaning of the Revolution. Politicians, radicals, artists, historians, teachers, businesspeople, and ordinary men and women have spent two centuries building up "new and improved" versions of the Founders—and then tearing them down to make way for what they think are even newer and more improved ones. The process continues today.

John Trumbull based his 1820 painting Declaration of Independence *(with John Adams, Roger Sherman, Robert R. Livingston, Thomas Jefferson, and Benjamin Franklin standing at center, left to right) on Jefferson's memory of the scene in Congress on July 4, 1776.*
Courtesy of the Yale University Art Gallery, Trumbull Collection.

How is it possible for people to disagree and change their minds so much about historical events, about figures from the past who died so long ago? Partly because the Founders themselves disagreed with one another, changed their minds, and harbored mixed feelings about what their own accomplishments meant. The revolutionaries left behind them a complex and sometimes contradictory record of achievements and opinions. Poring over their testimony, later Americans were able to pick and choose the version or aspect of Thomas Jefferson or George Washington that suited their own beliefs and arguments. Different Americans picked different versions. Time and again, "our" Jefferson has been pitted against "their" Jefferson.

Images and versions of the Founders also changed as America itself changed. As Americans moved from farms and villages to factories and cities, as they fought a bloody Civil War and two world wars to become the world's most powerful nation, they discovered new meanings in the Founding Fathers that previous generations had not seen. People managed to find ideas and qualities in the lives of George Washington, Benjamin Franklin, and other revolutionary heroes that seemed to mirror their own concerns and hopes—even if the Founders themselves might not always have understood or accepted how later Americans saw them.

Especially at times of upheaval—during wars, depressions, and political crises—the Founders are reassuring symbols of values worth holding on to and fighting for, principles of liberty and equality that ensure the survival of the nation. But equality for whom? What kind of liberty? Which Founders? Americans keep coming up with different answers to these questions.

For many, the meaning of the Founders could not be separated from their own struggles for freedom and equality. African-Americans, Native Americans, women, laborers, farmers, immigrants, reformers, and dissenters fought long and hard battles to win rights they believed the Founders had guaranteed in the Declaration of Independence and the Constitution. Often they struggled against others who remained convinced that the Founders had never intended equality for Americans who were not white, not male, not native born, not Protestant, not wealthy or middle-class. But as ever-greater numbers of Americans battled for and won their civil and political rights, they discovered their own Founding Fathers (and Founding Mothers), common people like themselves who had faced the redcoats alongside George Washington, or had dreamed with Tom Paine of independence. These forgotten, ordinary heroes of the Revolution became figures of inspiration and courage for Americans who had to fight for their share in the pursuit of happiness, while angering those who sought to keep things just as they were.

As countries go, the United States is a relatively young one. In searching for the nation's identity, Americans have not been able to turn to tales and myths of ancient kings and heroes, as Europeans, Asians, and Africans can.

The Founders serve that purpose for us, as parents of everything the nation has become and we are. But the United States was also the first nation in world history to be dedicated at its birth to the ideals of liberty and equal human rights. Those principles have remained vital to Americans, even as we continue to debate their meaning.

The Founders have come to symbolize more than just their own accomplishments and beliefs. What did the Philadelphia printer Benjamin Franklin or the Virginia lawyer Patrick Henry or the black seaman Crispus Attucks really stand for? This is another way of asking, What is America? What does it mean to be American? For this reason, the Founders refuse to lie dead and buried in school courses and textbooks. Because Americans continue to argue and disagree about the Founders and the nation they created, the revolutionaries remain living and breathing human beings.

Franklin, Washington, and the Rod

THE FOUNDERS IN THEIR OWN TIME

☞ *The Founders*

Benjamin Franklin, George Washington, and Thomas Jefferson belong on any list of the nation's founders. All three men understood the part they were playing in history. They took very seriously the idea that they would be studied as models of what the new American nation stood for. They tried to act as if their lives were lessons in leadership for Americans and the rest of the world.

But they could not always mold the opinions of others, or control what details of their personalities and which of their human flaws critics would exploit. While the American tradition of hero worship began at the nation's birth, so did the American tradition of slinging dirt and ripping apart the reputations of political leaders.

☞ *Autobiography of a Nation*

> *The History of our Revolution will be one continued Lye from one End to the other. The Essence of the whole will be that Dr. Franklins electrical Rod, Smote the Earth and out Sprung General Washington. That Franklin electrified him with his Rod—and thence forward these two conducted all the Policy Negotiations Legislation and War.*
>
> —*John Adams to Benjamin Rush, April 4, 1790*

Jealous John Adams parodied the way he thought future generations might remember the events of the American Revolution. His envy was understandable, for in the eyes of many people of his day, Benjamin Franklin *was* America. Printer, writer, self-made businessman, scientist, inventor, diplomat, states-man, revolutionary—his list of accomplishments seemed endless. In his own lifetime, Franklin enjoyed more international fame than any other American. In Europe his face was printed on vases, clocks, handkerchiefs, dishes, rings, and pocketknives, and sold to legions of admirers. On both sides of the At-lantic, his charm, wit, and flirtatiousness became legendary. "His friendship was delightful," a French acquaintance commented after Franklin's death, "a perfect good nature, a simplicity of manner . . . and above all a sweet serenity that easily turned into gaiety. Such was the society of this great man."

But the man who described himself as "kind, humane & benevolent Ben Franklin" worked hard to shape the way others saw him. Franklin had a genius for self-promotion. As his achievements brought him fame and influence, he also came to realize that he symbolized America to people around the world. Franklin not only sold himself, but now used his charm to further the cause of American independence and to promote the interests of his native country. In the coffeehouses and royal palaces of the Old World, Ben Franklin convinced Europeans that his virtues and talents were widely shared among the new peo-ple known as Americans.

The son of a humble Boston candle maker, he was apprenticed at age twelve to his older brother James, a printer. At seventeen, he rebelled against James's strictness by running away to Philadelphia, which would become his home. Franklin later reflected that his road to revolution started in his brother's printing shop: "I fancy his harsh & tyrannical Treatment of me, might be a means of impressing me with that Aversion to arbitrary Power that has stuck to me thro' my whole life."

Over the next three decades, Franklin became Philadelphia's most renowned citizen. He organized the city's first volunteer fire company, its li-brary, the Pennsylvania Hospital, and a school that became the University of Pennsylvania, and took action to ensure that the streets were clean and well lit. His thriving career as a printer made him one of the city's most successful businessmen. Franklin attributed his success to methodical habits and strict self-discipline. He avoided drinking and gambling, and sought to live by a list of thirteen virtues, which included industry, thrift, moderation, chastity, and cleanliness. In the publications that issued from his printing press, Franklin recommended this course to other Americans seeking fame and fortune. "I have always thought," he wrote, "that one Man of tolerable Abilities may work great Changes & accomplish great Affairs among Mankind, if he first forms a good Plan, and cutting off all Amusements or other Employments that would divert his Attention, makes the Execution of that same Plan his sole Study and Business."

Franklin was extremely proud of the self-control and hard work that allowed him to rise from "the Poverty & Obscurity in which I was born & bred, to a State of Affluence & some Degree of Reputation in the World." But he also knew the value of good advertising and the usefulness of selling himself. "I took care not only to be in *Reality* Industrious & frugal, but to avoid all *Appearances* of the Contrary. I drest plainly; I was seen at no Places of idle Diversion; I never went out a-fishing or shooting." To impress potential customers with his diligence, the young printer pushed his own supplies through the streets on a wheelbarrow rather than dispatch an apprentice to do it. "Thus being esteem'd an industrious thriving young Man . . . I went on swimmingly."

Winning friends and influencing people did not always come so naturally. As a young man Franklin was proud of his abilities to the point of arrogance. After a Quaker friend reproached him for being "overbearing & rather insolent," he decided to change his manner. He made sure to seem modest, conciliatory, even hesitant when presenting his views to others. In conversation with someone he knew to be wrong, "I deny'd myself the Pleasure of contradicting him abruptly," instead gently and gradually bringing him round to his own opinion. Franklin had learned that by telling people what they wanted to hear, he could get them to do what he wanted—a lesson he would remember for the rest of his career. But he never lost his vanity. He joked that if "I had compleatly overcome it, I should probably be proud of my Humility."

In person and in his writings, Franklin presented himself as an even-tempered, practical man who rarely became emotional or made mistakes. Like many Europeans and Americans during the eighteenth century's Age of Reason, Franklin believed he could perfect himself by bringing his emotions and flaws under the control of his rational mind. But beneath his public image lurked a more human, passionate Franklin, a person he usually tried to keep out of the public eye. He admitted in his *Autobiography*, first published one month after his death in 1790, that as a young unmarried man in Philadelphia, the "hard-to-be-govern'd Passion of Youth" drove him into sexual relations with "low Women." Indeed, Franklin had an illegitimate son, William, who, as royal governor of New Jersey during the Revolution, enraged his father by remaining loyal to England.

By the age of forty-two, Franklin's prosperity had enabled him to retire from his printing business and to devote his time to "Philosophical Studies and Amusements." His most famous discovery was that lightning was a form of electricity. Franklin sought to publicize his findings among the learned men of the Old World. But they could not take him seriously. Many Europeans viewed the thirteen American colonies as a primitive backwater inhabited by ignorant frontiersmen, hardly a place to generate new ideas. A French writer noted that "America has not yet produced a good poet, a capable mathematician, or a man of genius in a single art or a single science." Some European scientists even theorized that the North American climate reduced the intelligence and energy of settlers.

When Franklin's letters on electricity were first read in London's Royal Society, they were laughed at. It was only after French scientists, following his instructions, drew lightning to an iron rod before an astonished Paris crowd that Franklin's assertions were confirmed. Almost overnight, Franklin became the toast of the Western world. In the capital cities and universities of Europe, scientists and philosophers lauded him as an equal. Forced to admit its mistake, the Royal Society made him a member, as did the Royal Academy of Sciences in Paris. "He stole the fire of the Heavens and caused the arts to flower in savage climes," a French poet declared. "Greece would have set him among her gods."

★ FRANKLIN, WASHINGTON, AND THE ROD

As always, Franklin used the acclaim and eagerly played a new role: the wise philosopher of the transatlantic Enlightenment, a man at ease in the laboratories and royal courts of Europe. He had the painter David Martin portray him as a bewigged sage, deep in thought, with the bust of Sir Isaac Newton staring down approvingly upon him. Accounts of his own kite-flying experiment (conducted after Europeans had already proved his theory) strengthened the image of the practical, self-trained colonist whose achievements entitled him to be included among the world's great thinkers.

Franklin's scientific successes especially excited a circle of French intellectuals who championed America. Voltaire, Turgot, and other philosophers saw the British colonies of North America as "the hope of the human race," a place where society was starting all over again without the mistakes that Europe had made. The colonies, and particularly Franklin's own Pennsylvania, seemed free of the government repression, religious persecution, superstition, and poverty that shackled the Old World. The Pennsylvania farmer, they believed, was the freest, healthiest, happiest man in the world. On his hundred acres of land, Voltaire declared, the Pennsylvanian "is in truth king, for he is free and he is a citizen; he thinks what he pleases and he says what he pleases without being persecuted."

Benjamin Franklin's scientific achievements, the philosophers argued, proved their point. Pennsylvania, a land where people led simple, free, uncorrupted lives, had spawned a genius to equal the great thinkers of Europe. No one seemed to notice that Franklin was not a simple farmer but a sophisticated man who had lived practically all of his life in large cities. On his first two visits to Paris, in 1767 and 1769, Franklin shrewdly played to these perceptions. "The famous Franklin," a Paris periodical reported, "has told us that there is no working man in Pennsylvania who does not read the newspapers at lunch time and a few good works of philosophy or politics for an hour after dinner." Franklin was really describing himself, not the average Philadelphia laborer or

Franklin as scientific hero, stealing "the fire of the Heavens." Benjamin West's Franklin Drawing Electricity from the Sky, *1816.* Courtesy of the Philadelphia Museum of Art. Gift of Mr. and Mrs. Wharton Sinkler.

Benjamin Franklin as cultured sage of the Enlightenment, seated beneath a bust of Sir Isaac Newton. Portrait by David Martin, 1767. Courtesy of the Pennsylvania Academy of Fine Arts, Philadelphia. Gift of Marcia McKean Allen and Phebe Warren Downes through the bequest of their mother, Elizabeth Wharton McKean.

artisan. But he recognized that encouraging the French to envision America as a perfect society where every man was a philosopher might come in handy.

After taking part in the drafting of the Declaration of Independence, Franklin sailed for France in late 1776 as special envoy of the new United States. On his arrival in Paris, he was mobbed by enthusiastic well-wishers. He dined with leading intellectuals, posed for portraits, and flirted with court ladies, who vowed to use their influence in his behalf. "Your father's face [is] as well known as that of the moon," he wrote to his daughter Sarah. Over the next five years, he worked to drum up French support for the American cause.

Once again, he did so by manipulating his image. He gave up the powdered wig and elegant coat he had worn while posing for David Martin's portrait. Instead, he sported a fur cap, left his gray hair uncovered, and, in contrast to the uniformed courtiers and diplomats at Versailles, wore plain brown suits. As the natural genius from the woods and fields of America, he caused a sensation in Paris. His pose, symbolizing the simple virtues of a people fighting to keep their freedom, worked to spread pro-American feeling.

To counteract Franklin's influence, the British government sponsored publications for circulation in France that presented him in a very different light. One such periodical called him a "traitor to his king" and the "dean of all charlatans," who "deceived the good with his white hairs, and fools with his spectacles." But this kind of anti-Franklin and anti-American propaganda had little effect. The French had already taken the seventy-year-old Philadelphian to their hearts. Envisioning the homegrown scientist drawing lightning from the skies, one enthusiastic poet summed up French confidence in Franklin with a question: "Can he who has disarmed the gods fear the power of kings?"

Franklin used this popularity to fulfill his diplomatic mission. In negotiation with the French king's officials, he helped to secure recognition of the United States and obtained French troops and arms to aid the Continental Army, acts that ensured American independence.

"This is the Age of Experiments," Franklin commented in his *Autobiography*. On his deathbed in 1790, he could look back on a life immersed in many of his century's most momentous experiments, both scientific and political. He

BENJAMIN FRANKLIN.

Né à Boston, dans la nouvelle Angleterre le 17 Janvier 1706

had used all his political skill to labor for American independence in 1776 and a federal Constitution in 1787. He was now a symbol of what America was becoming—a society of ordinary men and women, confident in their own reason and industry, who were shaking off the limits and obstacles that European tradition had put in their way. "All that has happened to you is also connected with the detail of the manners and situation of *a rising* people," a friend had once told Franklin. It was Franklin's gift to see this, and to shape and reshape his image to benefit himself and the interests of his country.

☞ *The Most Beloved Man in America*

"Through all the land he appears like a benevolent god; old men, women, children they all flock eagerly to catch a glimpse of him when he travels and congratulate themselves because they have seen him." By 1781, when a French observer described him in this way, George Washington was already the most beloved man in America. When Washington accepted command of the Continental Army in June 1775, he automatically became a symbol of the American cause, the man upon whom patriots pinned their hopes. Cheering crowds mobbed him in Philadelphia and New York as he made his way north to the army's encampment outside Boston. As commander of a small, inexperienced army drawn from thirteen very different colonies challenging the world's most powerful military force, Washington stood for unity and courage in the face of adversity. By 1778, a Pennsylvania printer was already describing him in an almanac for German settlers as *des Landes Vater*, "the Father of His Country."

Like Franklin, Washington was acutely aware of the power and influence he exerted through his appearance and demeanor. While both men worked actively to make their images fit what people wanted and expected, Washington did not have to labor as hard as the wily Franklin. His natural reserve, dignity, and self-restraint appealed to a people looking for a leader they could trust with power.

Franklin as backwoods genius, complete with fur cap and spectacles. Line engraving by Augustus de Saint-Aubin, 1777. Courtesy of the Philadelphia Museum of Art, Rockefeller Collection.

To be sure, there were sides to Washington's personality that were less attractive, and he sought to keep these traits out of the public eye. As Thomas Jefferson put it, he was "inclined to gloomy apprehensions": He could be pessimistic and irritable, and he sometimes obsessively feared that he would die an early death, as his father and half-brother had. His emotional coolness put off some of his closest allies, including Alexander Hamilton, who once wrote that he had "a heart of stone." Faced with the challenge of commanding undisciplined troops during the Revolution, Washington sometimes gave in to despair and self-pity. "O how I wish I had never seen the Continental Army!" he once wrote privately. "I would have done better to retire to the back country and live in a wigwam." Some who knew him well felt that, for all his professed modesty, he was a vain man who cared too much how future generations would view him. But the Washington that most Americans saw was a colossal hero, the man who would win the Revolutionary War and guarantee the survival of the independent United States.

Washington certainly looked the part of a hero—or so, at least, Americans believed. "You would distinguish him to be a General and a Soldier, from among ten thousand people," the patriot Benjamin Rush noted reassuringly at the beginning of the war. Despite defective teeth and a pockmarked face—a reminder of the smallpox that had afflicted him at age nineteen—Washington had the bearing of a leader. At six feet two inches in height, he was some nine inches taller than the average eighteenth-century American man. "In conversation, he looks you full in the face," a fellow veteran of the French and Indian War commented. "His demeanor [is] at all times composed and dignified. His movements and gestures are graceful, his walk majestic, and he is a splendid horseman."

Sacred to the Memory of Washington *by John James Barralet, 1802. This engraving of George Washington ascending to heaven, made shortly after the first president's death, was so popular that it was copied by Chinese artists for sale in the United States during the heyday of the China trade.* Courtesy of the New York Public Library, Print Collection; Miriam and Ira D. Wallach Division of Art, Prints, and Photographs; Astor, Lenox, and Tilden Foundations.

Washington's personality even more than his looks convinced Americans of his greatness. "I beg it may be remembered, by every gentleman in this room, that I, this day, declare with the utmost sincerity, I do not think myself equal to the command I am honored with." With these words, Washington accepted command of the Continental Army from Congress in Philadelphia on June 16, 1775. His modesty impressed the assembled congressmen. The new general was "no harum starum ranting swearing fellow," one satisfied delegate remarked. Commentators had always noted his lack of egotism. When the Virginia House of Burgesses had honored the twenty-six-year-old colonel for his service against the French and Indians, Washington rose, "blushed, stammered, and trembled, for a second" before resuming his seat.

This was precisely the kind of commander Americans wanted. A people in rebellion feared arrogant, ambitious men who lusted after power. It was such men—not modest, reserved ones like Washington—who became tyrants, trampling on the rights of the people. The fact that Washington resigned his commission to Congress at the end of the war rather than be tempted into making himself military dictator (or king, as some of his officers wanted) proved that the people's rights were safe in his hands. Even the English king George III was impressed. In a conversation with the American-born artist Benjamin West during the war, the king had asked what Washington would do if the Americans won. West replied that Washington would probably retire to his farm rather than hold on to power. "If he does that," the king commented, "he will be the greatest man in the world."

The glorification of Washington intensified after he retired from his generalship to his plantation at Mount Vernon. Americans turned George Washington into an almost mythical figure, a superhero all citizens could idolize. Poets referred to him as the American Cincinnatus, recalling the hero of Roman legend who left his plow to defend his country from invaders, only to

Giuseppe Ceracchi's bust of George Washington, sculpted in a style to remind viewers of the statesmen of ancient Rome, was Thomas Jefferson's favorite portrait of "the father of his country." Courtesy of the Gibbes Museum of Art.

return to his farm after victory. Others compared him to Moses: "Our miraculous deliverer from a second Egypt—another house of bondage."

Many believed that, next to Jesus Christ, he was the greatest man who had ever lived. Ezra Stiles, president of Yale University, was typical of many enthusiasts. "O Washington! how do I love thy name!" he wrote. "Thy fame is of sweeter perfume than Arabian spices in the gardens of Persia. . . . Listening angels shall catch the odor, waft it to heaven, and perfume the universe!" Some, however, warned that excessive praise was blowing Washington out of proportion. "I respect our great general," one writer asserted, "but let us not make a GOD of him!"

Washington did not remain in retirement for long. As commanding officer during the war, he had been plagued by the disunity of the thirteen state governments and their refusal to cooperate with Congress and the Continental Army. When a number of revolutionary leaders began to voice their dissatisfaction with the state of affairs under the Articles of Confederation after the War, Washington expressed his own wishes for a stronger, more unified national government. It was natural that the man viewed as a second Moses would be chosen to preside at the Constitutional Convention in Philadelphia in 1787. Nor was it surprising that delegates based their visions of a new kind of executive officer, the president, on the character of the dignified, fifty-five-year-old Virginian who had led them to independence.

Washington faced his election to the presidency in 1788 with typical reluctance and self-doubt. He set out for his inauguration in New York, he wrote, with "feelings not unlike those of a culprit who is going to the place of his execution." He realized that the whole world was watching to see if the American experiment in self-government would succeed. On his own shoulders he felt the burden of proving false the idea that men were "unequal to the task of governing themselves and therefore made for a master."

The problem was how to go about doing it. Washington and his advisers had to figure out the most basic rules of presidential conduct and protocol, since no one had ever done so before. "I walk on untrodden ground," the first president remarked. Washington felt pulled in opposite directions as he defined the role he would play. On one hand, the elected leader of a free people had to avoid the pomp and luxury so beloved by the monarchs and royal courts of Europe; the American republic called for a simplicity of manner and dress in its chief executive. On the other hand, Alexander Hamilton, his secretary of the treasury and closest adviser, warned Washington not to go too far in shedding the trappings of the European kings. Hamilton and other conservatives thought that a people so recently stirred by revolution needed to be impressed by the dignity and majesty of their president in order to respect and obey him. If they didn't hold Washington in awe, they might even rebel again.

Washington thus had to appear both dignified and unassuming. His own modesty inclined him to prefer simplicity over ceremony. He was pleased when Congress agreed that his official title would be President of the United States rather than His Highness or His Supremacy, as some wanted. Under pressure from Hamilton and the vice president, John Adams, Washington did consent to appear at weekly levees, or receptions, like those hosted by kings, where he greeted visiting dignitaries. But, in his dresscoat with a sword hanging at his side, he always felt uncomfortable and self-conscious at these events. Hoping to make a quiet entrance, he was shocked at the first levee when his young aide David Humphreys ushered him into a room of expectant visitors by shouting, "The President of the United States." "Well, you have taken me in once," he blurted out angrily to Humphreys, "but by God, you will never take me in a second time!"

The president paid a price for his willingness to take part in such ceremonies. By 1793, when he began his second term, angry disagreement over whether the United States should support or oppose the French Revolution, along with disputes over domestic policy, had prompted the formation of two political parties, the Federalists and the Democratic-Republicans. Alexander Hamilton led the Federalists, while Secretary of State Thomas Jefferson headed the Democratic-Republicans. A distressed Washington tried to make peace between his two cabinet officers, while also seeking to remain above the fray. But as party animosity increased, the president was dragged in. When Washington remained neutral after England and France went to war, furious

LOOK ON THIS PICTURE,   AND ON THIS.

A Federalist print contrasts a heroic, manly George Washington with a scowling, shriveled, beady-eyed Thomas Jefferson, 1807. Courtesy of the collection of the New-York Historical Society.

Democratic-Republicans demanded to know why the president would not support France, the world's other budding revolutionary republic. Was he forgetting the people and becoming pro-British? Could his modesty truly withstand the kingly levees, the nationwide celebrations of his birthday? Was power finally going to Washington's head?

The man who, a few short years before, had been universally celebrated as a second Moses was now blasted in Democratic-Republican newspapers as a villain. "George I, Perpetual Dictator of the United States," was how a South

Carolina paper described him. Thomas Paine, a former ally, wrote a pamphlet denouncing him as "treacherous in private friendship . . . and a hypocrite in public life." Digging up forty-year-old misinformation, newspapermen accused him of murdering a captured French officer during the French and Indian War. His behavior during the presidential levees came under fire: The "distant and stiff" way he bowed proved that Washington was putting on the airs of a king. One editor even publicly wished for his "speedy death."

Washington was infuriated and hurt by the attacks. The fact that Federalist newspapers and politicians defended him was small consolation. Jefferson described to James Madison one cabinet meeting where the president, flying into a rage, swore that he regretted not resigning after his first term, "and that *by God* he had rather be in his grave than in his present situation. That he had rather be on his farm than to be made *emperor of the world*, and yet . . . they were charging him with wanting to be a king." Washington complained to Jefferson that the press was treating him "in such exaggerated and indecent terms as could scarcely be applied to a Nero, a notorious defaulter, or a common pickpocket."

Exhausted and embittered by the party battles he could not quell, Washington refused to run for a third term, although many Americans would have supported him as president for life. He told Hamilton that he would close his public career on March 4, 1797, the last day of his term, "after which no consideration under heaven that I can foresee shall again draw me from the walks of private life." With typical modesty, his Farewell Address to the American people included an apology for any mistakes he had made in office.

After his death in 1799, most of the accusations against him were forgotten. Now that he was gone, Washington became more and more godlike and perfect in eulogies, poems, and mass-produced prints. Then, a traveling bookseller and parson, Mason Weems, concocted a version of George Washington that would linger in the American mind for close to two centuries. Weems's book *The Life of Washington,* first published shortly after the president's death, dwelled on its subject's private life rather than his public career. In chapters devoted to Washington's childhood, Weems held him up to American readers as

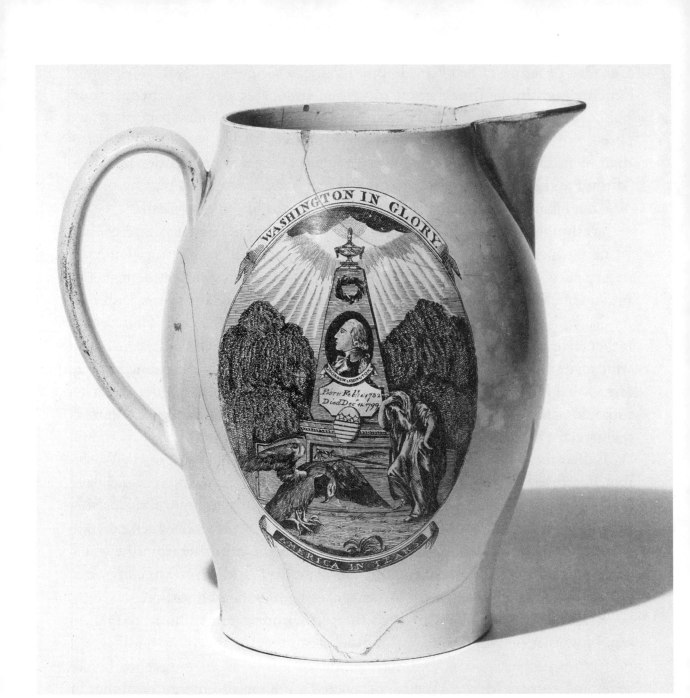

The selling of George Washington memorabilia was a thriving industry by the early nineteenth century. This pitcher glorifying Washington, along with other patriotic pottery intended for sale in the United States, was actually manufactured in the "mother country"—England. Courtesy of the National Museum of American History, Political History Collection.

a model of honesty and goodness—indeed, young George was a perfect human being. In the fifth edition, printed in 1806, Weems added a memorable example of the six-year-old Washington's character:

> "George," *said his father,* "do you know who killed that beautiful little cherry-tree yonder in the garden?" *This was a* tough question; *and George staggered under it for a moment; but quickly recovered himself: and looking at his father, with the sweet face of youth brightened with the inexpressible charm of all-conquering truth, he bravely cried out,* "I can't tell a lie, Pa; you know I can't tell a lie. I did cut it with my hatchet."

Weems's book was so popular that it went through eighty editions and was still being printed in 1929. His examples of Washington's virtues were widely reprinted in school textbooks. But Weems, who was something of a con man, invented the cherry-tree story, along with other biographical anecdotes. The author's main goal was to boost the sale of his book; there was "a great deal of money lying in the bones of old George," he slyly told his publisher. Some of Weems's contemporaries realized that his stories sounded like tall tales. One acquaintance noted that the problem with his books was that "you know not how much of fiction there is in them."

But this didn't matter to millions of American readers. People needed a Washington who had been the best and bravest man in the world, a strong, reassuring father who symbolized every good quality Americans hoped to find in themselves. The blushing, self-doubting soldier had become a hero so immense that his very humanity seemed lost in birthday parades and cherry-tree stories.

☞ *Wise Tom and Dusky Sally*

In 1825 Thomas Jefferson gave his grandson the small portable writing desk on which he had drafted the Declaration of Independence some forty-nine years earlier. "Politics as well as Religion has its superstitions," Jefferson wrote to him. "These, gaining strength with time, may one day, give imaginary value to this relic, for its association with the birth of the Great Charter of our Independence."

Jefferson realized that future generations would look back on the drafting of the Declaration as the moment of their nation's birth. He also knew that he and other Founding Fathers would be honored, and possibly even revered as superhuman heroes. Jefferson scoffed at the inflated "imaginary value" future Americans would place on the leaders and artifacts of the Revolution. But in his own lifetime Jefferson did not undervalue the power and influence his role as revolutionary gave him. He understood that he could use the way people saw him to shape the kind of society he wanted the fledgling United States to be.

Thomas Jefferson was a complex man. Shy and hypersensitive to criticism, plagued by agonizing week-long headaches when under stress, he cherished the privacy and tranquillity of his beloved mountaintop home at Monticello, Virginia. He hated having to speak in public. John Adams, his fellow delegate in the Continental Congress during the Revolution, later described him as "the most silent man in Congress. . . . I never heard him utter three sentences together" in debate. Jefferson felt much more suited to the "tranquil pursuits of science" than to the strains and conflicts of political life. Yet he immersed himself in the Revolution. By the time he was elected president in 1800, he had been wartime governor of Virginia, represented the new United States as its minister to France, served as the first secretary of state, and written Virginia's landmark act guaranteeing religious freedom, as well as drafted the Declaration of Independence.

His life was a bundle of contradictions. An amateur scientist and naturalist, inventor, scholar, and one of the fathers of American architecture, Jeffer-

Jefferson's supporters saw him as the Sage of Monticello, equally at home in the realms of science, the arts, and politics. The artist Cornelius Tiebout portrayed the new president in 1801 holding the Declaration of Independence while standing between laboratory equipment and the bust of another Renaissance man, Benjamin Franklin. Courtesy of the Library of Congress, LC-USZ 62-75384.

son seemed most comfortable viewing himself as a plain gentleman farmer. He championed the common people of America, especially the "cultivators of the earth," who, he felt, were the best guardians of American liberty and independence. "I am not among those who fear the people," he wrote. "They, and not the rich, are our dependence for continued freedom." But he was also one of the most sophisticated men in the country, a wealthy intellectual who loved Europe's artistic riches and lamented the fact that music, "the favorite passion of my soul," was "in a state of deplorable barbarism" in America. Above all he valued liberty and "the natural equality of man." Yet he lived off the labor of some two hundred black slaves.

It was as president that Jefferson realized the power he exerted through his appearance—an appearance that surprised and even shocked some of his contemporaries. On March 4, 1801, his first day as president, Jefferson, dressed in a plain suit, walked from the boardinghouse where he was staying to the Senate Chamber in the Capitol to deliver his Inaugural Address. His two predecessors, George Washington and John Adams, attired in elegant dresscoats with ceremonial swords, had traveled to their inaugurations in lavish horse-drawn carriages. Throughout his presidency, when Jefferson welcomed visitors to the White House he often greeted them dressed in a threadbare coat, a white shirt that needed laundering, a favorite red vest, corduroy knee breeches, and worn-out slippers. A disgusted British diplomat, expecting more dignity from the president of the United States, sneered that Jefferson looked like "a tall large-boned farmer." But another English visitor, impressed by his casual manner, defended him as "an enemy to luxury and parade."

To be sure, Jefferson lacked the stately bearing of a Washington. "His clothes seem too small for him," one observer noted when Jefferson appeared as secretary of state before a Senate committee. "He sits in a lounging Manner on one hip, commonly, and with one of his shoulders elevated much above the other. . . . His whole figure has a loose shackling Air. He had a rambling Vacant look and nothing of that firm collected deportment which I expected would dignify the presence of a Secretary."

Jefferson fashioned his appearance carefully. He knew that through word-of-mouth and newspaper reports, people in America and Europe would come to see him as a leader who scorned all pomp and pride. Jefferson wanted his presidency to stand for everything that Washington's and Adams's had not. He had once been on friendly terms with both men, but the political quarrels of the 1790s had ended that. Jefferson felt that his two predecessors had sold out the Revolution by elevating the presidency beyond the reach of ordinary citizens. In effect, they had mimicked the glittering royal courts of Europe, where human "lions, tygers, hyaenas, and other beasts of prey" lorded it over the common people.

As leader of the emerging Democratic-Republican Party in the 1790s, Jefferson had come to believe that wealthy Federalist merchants and bankers in Boston, Philadelphia, and New York—egged on by his enemy Alexander Hamilton—wanted to transform the United States into an aristocratic state or a monarchy, complete with the distinctions between privileged noblemen and common people that prevailed in England. With their formal levees and presidential wardrobes, Jefferson felt, Washington and Adams had played into Hamilton's hands. Just like the kings of Europe who crushed liberty by taxing their subjects into poverty, the first two presidents had spent too much of the people's money on frivolous and vain ceremonies. Only small government and low taxes, he felt, would preserve American freedom. He saw it as his mission to show that an unassuming, frugal man could and should hold the highest office in the nation.

A man of Jefferson's tastes could not play this role all the time. At the White House dinners he hosted for members of Congress and visiting dignitaries, he dressed elegantly and prided himself on the expensive gourmet meals and fine wines served by his hand-picked French chef. Yet here, too, Jefferson made the point that in a republic, equal rights were the rule. Instead of sending out invitations as president of the United States, he simply signed them with his customary "Th: Jefferson." Unlike the European royal courts, where officials were seated according to their rank and title, Jefferson permitted his guests to seat themselves "pell mell," which meant wherever it suited them (with the exception that women seated themselves before men).

Jefferson sought to present himself to the American people as a down-to-earth man who respected only one aristocracy—a "natural aristocracy" of talented and virtuous men who could be found as frequently among the poor and middle-class as among the rich. For the Democratic-Republican voters who supported and reelected him, this image was a persuasive one. But in the eyes of his Federalist enemies, who viewed him as a reckless and foolhardy radical, the image was a false one that had to be shattered.

Federalist newspapermen and pamphleteers claimed to uncover a very different Jefferson. They ridiculed his scientific interests as the foolish hobbies of an addle-brained visionary, and argued that his celebrated modesty was the pose of a mean-spirited hypocrite who really despised the people. One Federalist newspaper ran a mock version of Jefferson's daily diary:

10 o'clock. Wrote half a page of my dissertation on cockroaches—servant came in to say, people below wanted to see me on public business—cursed their impertinence—sent word, I was out. . . .

12 o'clock . . . Ordered my horse—never ride with a servant—looks proud— mob doesn't like it—must gull [fool] *the boobies.*

The same "diary" had Jefferson blasting a prominent Federalist judge as "a sneering son of a bitch." Even the president's physical attributes came under fire. While Democratic-Republicans complimented him on his "clear and penetrating eye," Federalists detected the "shifty glance" of a power-hungry intriguer. When Jefferson, the self-proclaimed advocate of small government, enhanced federal power by purchasing the Louisiana Territory from France and declaring an embargo on all foreign trade during the Napoleonic Wars, his enemies labeled him "King Thomas." Attacking Jefferson's expressed doubts about the truth of conventional Christianity, Federalists declared that he was a dangerous atheist who was going to have all Bibles confiscated and burned.

But it was the assertions about his private life, made by a mentally unstable journalist named James Callender, that most enraged Jefferson and his allies. Callender had originally been a Democratic-Republican. After convincing himself that Jefferson mistreated and ignored him, the newspaperman took vengeance by offering his services to the Federalists.

In his Richmond *Recorder,* Callender reported a scandal involving the widower Jefferson and Sally Hemings, one of his Monticello slaves. After supposedly interviewing several of Jefferson's Virginia neighbors, Callender asserted that "the man, *whom it delighteth the people to honor,* keeps and for many years has kept, as his concubine, one of his slaves. Her name is SALLY. The name of her eldest son is Tom. His features are said to bear a striking though sable resemblance to those of the president himself. . . . By this wench Sally, our president has had several children."

In confidential letters to friends, Jefferson cursed Callender as "a damn'd rascal" and "a lying renegade." But the damage was done. Federalists throughout the country gleefully repeated the story about "Dusky Sally." In their eyes, the real Jefferson—not the shrewd politician who pretended to be a man of integrity—stood exposed before the American people. At a time when some Americans were beginning to question the place of slavery in a revolutionary republic, the president turned out to be worse than merely a self-indulgent lecher. He was also a hypocrite who spouted eloquent phrases about liberty while continuing to own—and sexually exploit—other human beings.

Federalist papers published a satirical version of "Yankee Doodle," claiming tongue in cheek that Jefferson himself sang it in the White House:

> *Of all the damsels on the green,*
> *On mountain, or in valley,*
> *A lass so luscious ne'er was seen,*
> *As Monticellian Sally*
>
> *Yankee doodle, who's the noodle?*
> *What wife were half so handy?*
> *To breed a flock of slaves for stock,*
> *A blackamoor's the dandy.*

When press'd by loads of state affairs
I seek to sport and dally
The sweetest solace of my cares
Is in the lap of Sally.

Fearing that any reference on his part to Callender's story would merely fan its flames, Jefferson kept silent. He left it to his own party's editors to blast Callender and other Federalist scandalmongers as unprincipled liars. But, as George Washington had found out before him, the wounds opened by political accusation did not heal quickly. For the rest of his life he remained bitterly angry at the treatment he had received at the hands of his enemies. "Nothing can now be believed which is seen in a newspaper," he wrote to an acquaintance in 1807, during his second presidential term. "Truth itself becomes suspicious by being put into that polluted vehicle." Two hundred years later, historians are still arguing over the truth or falsehood of the "Dusky Sally" story.

Jefferson's supporters continued to brush off the mud flung by critics after he retired from the presidency in 1809. To his admirers he became the Sage of Monticello, a multifaceted genius equally at home in the fields of architecture, natural science, educational innovation, and political thought. They agreed with his French friend the Chevalier de Chastellux, to whom it seemed as though "he had placed his mind, like his house, on a lofty height, whence he might contemplate the whole universe."

Jefferson relished his retirement from politics at Monticello. But in private and public letters he continued to spread his vision of an America dedicated to life, liberty, and equality for the common farmer as well as the wealthy businessman. Invited to attend ceremonies in Washington, D.C., on the occasion of the fiftieth anniversary of the signing of the Declaration of Independence, he politely declined, citing illness. But he did regard with satisfaction the influence his Revolution was continuing to exert around the world. "All eyes are opened or opening to the rights of man," he wrote. "The mass of mankind has not been born with saddles on their backs, nor a favored few booted and spurred, ready to ride them legitimately, by the grace of God."

To the end, Jefferson sought to shape how his fellow Americans would view him. He left careful instructions specifying the epitaph to be inscribed on his tombstone at Monticello, so future generations would remember him as he wished to be remembered. Typically, he did not mention the power he had held as president of the United States. Instead, he listed the three accomplishments he was most proud of, deeds that he believed had helped his fellow citizens to preserve their freedom and pursue happiness:

Here was buried
THOMAS JEFFERSON
Author of the Declaration of American Independence
of the Statute of Virginia for religious freedom
and Father of the University of Virginia.

Franklin, Washington, and Jefferson all tried to shape how their countrymen and the world would see them. To a large extent, they succeeded. Franklin shrewdly advertised himself as a successful businessman, an enlightened scientist, and a natural American genius in order to get what he wanted. Washington played the role of modest commander to reassure the American people that he did not lust for power. Jefferson presented himself to his country as a simple, down-to-earth president who avoided all luxury. None of these roles was false; each image matched some quality in the personalities of the three men. But each individual was also more complex, more human than these images suggested. While Franklin died too soon to become embroiled in the bitter party battles of the 1790s and 1800s, Washington and Jefferson both had the experience of seeing themselves glorified by their supporters as great heroes and attacked by their enemies as villains and fools. Both men learned a lesson that would continue to hold true in the future, as later Americans continued to debate the meaning of the Revolution: There could be no single version of the lives of men who had founded a new nation, dedicated in principle to equality, liberty, and the pursuit of happiness.

Did Anybody Ever See Washington Naked?

THE ERA OF JACKSONIAN DEMOCRACY

☞ *Who Can Tell How Many Franklins May Be Among You?*

On the afternoon of July fourth, 1826, John Adams lay dying in his home at Quincy, Massachusetts. The ninety-year-old former president found comfort in one of his final thoughts, expressed to those gathered around him: "Thomas Jefferson still survives." The two men, foes during the party battles of the early republic, had become friends again late in life. But Adams was wrong. The eighty-three-year-old Jefferson had died five hours earlier in his bed at Monticello in Virginia. On the fiftieth anniversary of the Declaration of Independence, America lost two of the men most responsible for securing that independence and creating the United States.

Few Americans felt that the two deaths were coincidental. By taking away the two Founders together, many claimed, God was telling Americans that He approved of their experiment in liberty after fifty years of independence. But the deaths of Adams and Jefferson sent a more down-to-earth message as well: The generation that had fought the Revolution and created the republic was passing. Six years later, the last living signer of the Declaration, Charles Carroll of Maryland, died at the age of ninety-five.

A new and different America was emerging as the last of the Founders passed away. Common Americans—farmers, artisans, shopkeepers, and laborers—were gaining rights and opportunities that had previously belonged only to the rich and "well-born." Andrew Jackson of Tennessee, the man Americans elected president in 1828, symbolized many of these changes. Jackson was the first president born in poverty, and the first to come from the western frontier. He was also the first "self-made man" to become president. From extremely humble beginnings, Jackson rose to wealth and power as a prominent lawyer and businessman, a military hero during the War of 1812, and a politician of national importance.

Andrew Jackson's rise reflected the hopes and expectations of many "common" people. Throughout the country, workers and farmers took advantage of new opportunities to get ahead. New land on the frontier attracted families seeking a better life. In the seaport cities, industrious clerks hoped to become wealthy merchants, and young journeymen artisans looked forward to the day when they would be master craftsmen. One Founding Father, Benjamin Franklin, served as a role model for these young men. A New Yorker summed up the spirit of the era when he addressed a group of apprentices with a hopeful question: "Who can tell how many Franklins may be among you?"

The 1820s were also a period of political reform. Old laws that had kept poor men from voting were eliminated in state after state. Now all adult white males, regardless of how much property they owned, had the right to elect their representatives and to run for office themselves. Although women, slaves, many free blacks, and Indians remained excluded from the political system, the empowerment of all white men, rich or poor, struck many as a dramatic step forward in the expansion of freedom and equality.

Many of the Founding Fathers had expected poor and middle-class people to "stay in their place." As men of inherited wealth and power, most revolutionary leaders did not think that the poor could or should govern, and they felt it was unwise for "humble" men to rise too rapidly in society. Even Thomas Jefferson had resisted giving the vote to the very poor.

Yet Americans in this new "Age of the Common Man" continued to celebrate the Founding Fathers. In holiday parades and political rallies, artisans and workers proudly carried banners and rode floats decorated with the faces of George Washington and Benjamin Franklin. Speech makers at Fourth of July barbecues reminded their fellow citizens of the sacrifices made by the "heroes of '76."

★ DID ANYBODY EVER SEE WASHINGTON NAKED?

The lively way nineteenth-century Americans celebrated the Fourth of July—with men and women, adults and children, and blacks and whites mingling in the open air—is summed up in John Lewis Krimmel's watercolor Independence Day Celebration in Centre Square, 1819. *Note the picture of George Washington over the tent at left.* Courtesy of the Historical Society of Pennsylvania.

Ben Franklin as fireman. Young urban artisans and laborers joined volunteer fire companies to prove their prowess and enjoy one another's comradeship. Franklin—who had started Philadelphia's first fire company—became a working-class hero, as in this portrait painted by Charles Washington Wright about 1850. Courtesy of the CIGNA Museum and Art collection.

This was not surprising. After all, the ideas that the Founders had fought for—independence, liberty, the pursuit of happiness—continued to inspire Americans. But Americans were giving those ideas new meanings. Men who worked with their hands now staked their claim to the freedoms and rights the revolutionaries had fought for.

Inspired by the Revolution, other groups also began to press for rights that all human beings were supposed to share. African-Americans and women struggled against racism and sexual discrimination to redefine and expand the meaning of liberty and equality so that they, too, could enjoy the achievements of the Revolution. In each case, people looked back to the actions and ideas of the Founding Fathers to help them stake their claim to a free and equal place in the American republic.

☞ Man Worship

America's love affair with George Washington continued, even though the first president had been dead since 1799. Pictures and statues of Washington could be found everywhere—in galleries, public buildings, and private homes. Hundreds of published biographies, poems, plays, and schoolbooks celebrated his valor and statesmanship. Americans saw Washington as a symbol of what was best in the country and best in themselves. Proclaiming that Washington had been one of the greatest men who ever lived, Americans built up their national self-confidence in a world still dominated by the age-old monarchies of Europe.

Popular enthusiasm for Washington was so strong that it sometimes got out of hand. In an 1856 equivalent of a rock concert, hundreds of ticketless New Yorkers rushed the doorkeepers and crowded the aisles of a theater to hear a sold-out speech on "The Character of Washington."

Some Americans, however, were offended by this kind of enthusiasm for Washington. They worried that too much devotion to any political leader,

The Declaration of Independence sells suits. William Brown, a Philadelphia merchant, rewrote the Declaration to serve his own purposes in this advertisement from the 1830s.
Courtesy of the collection of the New-York Historical Society.

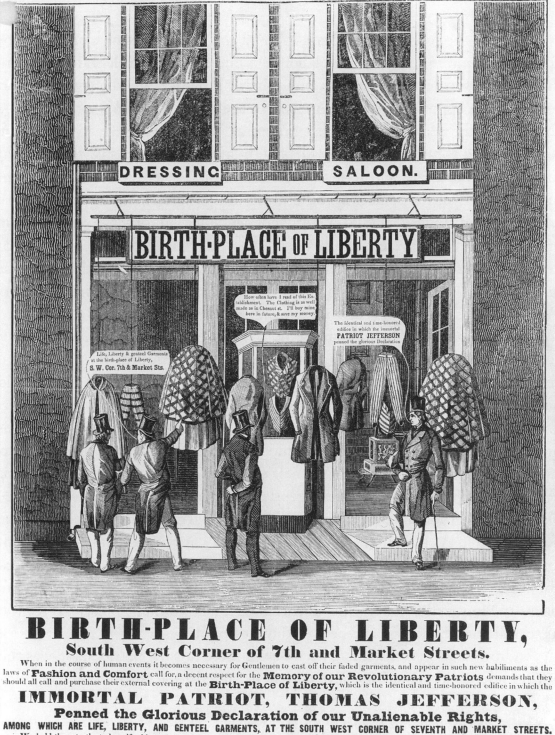

BIRTH-PLACE OF LIBERTY,
South West Corner of 7th and Market Streets.

When in the course of human events it becomes necessary for Gentlemen to cast off their faded garments, and appear in such new habiliments as the laws of **Fashion and Comfort** call for, a decent respect for the **Memory of our Revolutionary Patriots** demands that they should all call and purchase their external covering at the **Birth-Place of Liberty**, which is the identical and time-honored edifice in which the

IMMORTAL PATRIOT, THOMAS JEFFERSON,
Penned the Glorious Declaration of our Unalienable Rights,
AMONG WHICH ARE LIFE, LIBERTY, AND GENTEEL GARMENTS, AT THE SOUTH WEST CORNER OF SEVENTH AND MARKET STREETS.

We hold these truths to be self-evident, that men are treated equal—that they can obtain Clothing, as rich, as cheap, and as durable as at any other establishment in the nation, either by the dozen or single garment. Under the circumstances of this particular case, and in these days of humbug, it becomes necessary to state that 15 years' experience, and an ample cash capital, to make selections and purchases, will carry us out in what we assert. The style and workmanship is well known by the public, and the very low prices is every day becoming more notorious. Our shelves are now filled with the choicest collection of Fashionable Ready-made Clothing, consisting of Boys' as well as Mens' Cloaks, Oversacks, Sack Coats, Monkey Jackets, Business Sacks, Frock Sacks, Catalonia Cloaks, Dress and Frock Coats, Pantaloons and Vests.

even a dead one, was un-American. In 1832 the two houses of Congress created a joint committee to make elaborate arrangements to celebrate the hundredth anniversary of Washington's birth. But five of the twenty-nine congressmen appointed refused to serve. In the words of one Virginia senator, "Man worship"—even for so great a man as Washington—was wrong. Let Americans celebrate their dead leaders with lavish and expensive ceremonies, these critics reasoned, and soon enough they would start rewarding their living politicians in the same way. Surely, the five congressmen argued, Americans had not fought the War for Independence in order to treat their presidents as if they were kings or gods!

Others were frustrated that Washington was treated as if he had been made of marble. In the 1840s, after decades of paintings and poems that depicted Washington as perfect in everything he did, the novelist Nathaniel Hawthorne complained that the Great Man hardly seemed human at all. "Did anybody ever see Washington naked?" Hawthorne asked sarcastically. "It is inconceivable. He has no nakedness, but I imagine was born with his clothes on and his hair powdered, and made a stately bow on his first appearance in the world."

Washington, however, was not the only revolutionary veteran people celebrated. As America became more democratic, writers and historians tried to preserve a record of the forgotten heroes of the war, the common foot soldiers. Washington, Jefferson, and other "gentlemen" had led the struggle for independence, but thousands of ordinary farmers and artisans had done the fighting and dying. As the number of living Revolutionary War veterans dwindled, journalists fanned out to interview old men and publish their reminiscences about the war years. Even the aging Isaac Jefferson, one of Thomas Jefferson's slaves at Monticello, was tracked down so his image could be preserved for the historical record through the new medium of photography.

Andrew Jackson himself had been one of these unsung patriots. He was the last president old enough to have played any role in the Revolution. As a boy

Isaac Jefferson, blacksmith and former slave of Thomas Jefferson, photographed in Petersburg, Virginia, approximately 1845. Courtesy of the Tracy W. McGregor Library, Special Collections Department, University of Virginia Library.

A fourteen-year-old Andrew Jackson bravely wards off a blow from a British officer's saber in this popular nineteenth-century Currier & Ives print. Courtesy of the Library of Congress, LC-USZ 62-2340.

in the backwoods of North and South Carolina, he had fought in a skirmish against the redcoats and was taken prisoner. When Jackson refused to clean a British officer's boots, the enraged officer slashed him on the hand and head with a saber. Jackson bore these patriotic scars for the rest of his life—as his campaign managers reminded voters before each election.

☛ *On Strike for Freedom*

There was another side, though, to the "Age of Jackson." Many Americans remained without the rights and liberties that politicians boasted about in Fourth of July speeches. African-Americans, women, and even many white male workers lived without the opportunities that the Revolution had promised to bring. For these people, the Age of the Common Man was really an age of inequality. To some, it seemed that the expansion of democracy had only given more power to those who already possessed it.

Among those who felt cheated were men and women laboring in the nation's factories and workshops. By the 1820s, industrial mills for the manufacture of textiles, shoes, iron, and other goods were being built throughout New England and the mid-Atlantic states. This Industrial Revolution enriched the merchants and master craftsmen who owned the factories, but many of the mill hands worked long hours at monotonous jobs for low wages. Many workers feared the loss of their dignity. Factory owners, they felt, treated them like "wage slaves" rather than respecting them as equals.

This was the case at Lowell, Massachusetts, where a small group of wealthy merchants built an elaborate complex of cotton textile mills. Overseers recruited young women from farms all over New England to run the power looms that wove cloth in these mills. Initially, the "mill girls" earned high wages, and many flocked to Lowell in order to help their parents financially, to save up for a wedding dowry, or to find a more independent life for themselves.

The factory owners congratulated themselves on fulfilling the promise of the American Revolution. Not only were they providing jobs (while increasing their own wealth), they were also giving American consumers an alternative to buying cotton cloth imported from the factories of Great Britain. By creating a domestic textile industry, they were increasing America's economic independence from the former mother country.

Growing numbers of "mill girls," however, disagreed with their employers. When the Lowell industrialists announced wage cuts in 1834, eight hundred women went on strike. They voiced their own, very different understanding of the American Revolution. Among the strikers were granddaughters of the farmers who had started the Revolution by fighting as "minutemen" at Lexington and Concord in 1775. In a leaflet they circulated to explain their cause, the strikers argued that their "Patriotic Ancestors" had risked their lives "to procure independence for their children," not in order to have their grandchildren become the "slaves" of arrogant and greedy factory owners.

The Lowell strike failed. The owners ignored the arguments of strikers, and workers who refused to accept lower wages left the mills. But the anger expressed at Lowell was shared by other factory workers, who established labor unions to protect their wages and to improve working conditions. Laborers throughout New England and the Mid-Atlantic states saw the American Revolution as *their* struggle, one that they continued to fight against a new set of tyrants. When factory owners attacked unions by claiming that they were illegal conspiracies, one union organizer had a ready reply for them: The Founding Fathers themselves were "on a strike" against Great Britain when they had adopted the Declaration of Independence. By claiming that the Founders would have been on their side, striking workers proudly asserted that their struggle was a patriotic fight for liberty, equality, and justice.

☞ *Common Sense*

Some working men and women found their own Founding Father in Thomas Paine, one of the most controversial figures of the American Revolution. Paine started out as an unlikely hero. Born in England in 1737, he was trained to be an artisan staymaker—that is, a craftsman who made supports (or "stays") for women's corsets out of whalebone. After a stint working as a tax collector for the English government, Paine immigrated to the American colonies in 1774 and settled in Philadelphia. There he immersed himself in the revolutionary movement, and began a new career as a writer defending American rights.

Paine became famous practically overnight in January 1776 when he wrote and published a pamphlet entitled *Common Sense.* It immediately became a best-seller. By that time, the thirteen colonies had been at war with Great Britain for almost nine months, but the Continental Congress held back from declaring independence. While some revolutionaries demanded that the link between colonies and mother country be severed, many hesitated; a century and a half of American loyalty to English kings and queens seemed too meaningful a heritage to throw away so abruptly.

In *Common Sense,* Paine helped Americans to change their minds. In bold and uncompromising language, he argued that America must completely throw off its allegiance to George III. Only as citizens of thirteen independent republics, not as colonists, could Americans secure their rights. To hammer home his point, Paine did more than merely attack the British crown: He blasted the very idea of hereditary monarchy wherever it existed. "Of more worth is one honest man to society, and in the sight of God," he wrote, "than all the crowned ruffians that ever lived."

These were radical and unsettling ideas in a world dominated by monarchs and princes. But Americans were ready for Paine's ideas. Months of war and years of anti-British agitation had brought them to the brink of independence; Paine's eloquence gave them the final push. As it was reprinted in colony after colony and passed from hand to hand, *Common Sense* excited hundreds of thousands of readers. *Common Sense* became the most widely circulated publication ever to appear in America up to that point, and one of the greatest best-sellers of all time; with over one hundred thousand pamphlets in print within three months, one copy was sold for every twenty-five people living in the colonies. Paine could lay claim to being a Founding Father even though he was not a member of Congress: His pamphlet helped to provoke the debate that resulted in the Declaration of Independence.

After the Revolution, Paine's political ideas and writings became increasingly controversial. He moved back to Europe—first to London, then to Paris—and involved himself in a second great revolution, that of the French people in 1789 against their corrupt and oppressive monarchy. He wrote a new essay, *The Rights of Man,* that applauded the French revolutionaries for trying to create a representative government that protected the rights of their people. "It is an age of revolutions," Paine wrote happily, "in which everything may be looked for."

Paine found that the religious ideas of many of the French revolutionaries accorded with his own, and he wrote another pamphlet, *The Age of Reason,* to explain these ideas. Paine and his friends were Deists, or "freethinkers." Instead of seeking evidence of God's power and goodness in the Bible, they found it in the beauty and orderliness of the natural world God had created. Deists rejected Christianity, with its belief in saints and miracles, as a superstitious faith out of place in a modern world of enlightened men.

The Age of Reason became a manifesto for Deists both in Europe and America. In it Paine attempted to convince his readers that the "stupid Bible

Two versions of Thomas Paine: John Wesley Jarvis's 1806 portrait from life (above), and a 1791 English caricature by James Gillray, which portrays Paine as an evil imp whose radical ideas stirred up trouble on both sides of the Atlantic. Above: courtesy of the National Gallery of Art, Washington, D.C. Gift

of Marian B. Maurice. Right: courtesy of the American Philosophical Society Library, Philadelphia, Pennsylvania.

"These are your Gods, O, Israel!"

"Fathom & a half! Fathom & a half! Poor Tom!"

mercy upon me! that's more by half than my poor Measure will ever
ble to reach! - Lord, Lord, I wish I had a bit of the Stay-tape or Buckram which
ust to Cabbage when I was prentice, to lengthen it out; - well, well, who would
have thought it, that I, who have served Seven Years as an Apprentice, & afterwards
ed Four Years as a Journeyman to a Master Taylor, then follow'd the business of an
iseman as much longer, should not be able to take the dimensions of this Bauble! for what
rown but a Bauble? which we may see in the Tower for six pence apiece? - well altho
y be too large for a Taylor to take Measure of, there's one Comfort he may make mouths
call it as many names as he pleases! - and yet, Lord, Lord, I should like to make it a
-doodle Night Cap & Breeches, if it was not not so damn'd large, or I had stuff enough
could once do that, I would soon stitch up the mouth of that Barnacled Edmund
making of any more Reflections upon the Flints - & so Flint & Liberty
for ever - & damn the Dungs

Pub.d May 23.th 1791. by H.Humphrey
N.o 18, Old Bond Street

"THE RIGHTS OF MAN; - or TOMMY PAINE, the
little American Taylor, taking the Measure of the CROWN, for a new Pair of
Revolution-Breeches.

of the Church" was a source of ignorance and misinformation. Only science, the study of the laws governing nature, yielded "true theology."

Rather than winning him great praise, however, *The Age of Reason* made Paine one of the most hated men in the Western world. While Paine saw the French Revolution as a liberating event, conservatives in Europe and America came to regard it as a disaster. They pointed to the increasingly radical and violent measures taken by the revolutionary leaders: the beheading of the French king, bloody massacres of aristocrats and dissenters, attacks launched by Deists against the Church and Christian worship.

In America, leaders of the Federalist Party feared that the revolutionary "disease" unleashed in Paris might become contagious. They worried that the American spirit of rebelliousness that had helped win independence from Britain might be stirred up again in new and dangerous ways. Revolutionary fervor and the love of liberty could be taken *too* far. Infected by radical ideas, common farmers and artisans might rise in rebellion against the rich and the clergy, as they had done in France. This was especially true, Federalists felt, because Thomas Jefferson and his Democratic-Republicans were largely sympathetic to the ideals of the French revolutionaries. In their pamphlets, Federalists warned that Jefferson's "swinish multitude" might soon start a new revolution in America, burning Bibles in huge bonfires and setting up guillotines to behead wealthy gentlemen.

As author of the *The Rights of Man* and *The Age of Reason,* Paine became a choice target for the fear and hatred of Federalist conservatives. Federalist newspapermen and speech makers caricatured him as a bloodthirsty cutthroat, even though he had publicly opposed the execution of the French king. They described him as the "infidel Tom Paine," an "Apostle of the Devil" who hated all social order and religion. Even his personal habits, including a problem with alcohol, came under fire. To humiliate Paine, one editor claimed that, while staying in a Philadelphia boardinghouse, the pamphleteer had gotten drunk and urinated all over his landlady's "clean linen . . . which she had kept nicely starched out for high days and holidays."

When Paine returned to America from France in 1802, he was greeted by less than a hero's welcome. Too many Americans feared his ideas. His attacks on Christianity in *The Age of Reason* infuriated devout Americans of all social classes. Even Paine's old friend President Jefferson distanced himself from the man who, as much as any other, had set the stage for the Declaration of Independence. Thomas Paine, the writer who had dared thirteen colonies to dream of an independent United States, died poor and neglected on the outskirts of New York City in 1809.

More than a decade after his death, however, groups of working men and women began a Paine revival. Paine's birthday, January 29, became an occasion for annual celebrations by artisans and laborers in New York, Philadelphia, Boston, Cincinnati, and other cities. In 1834, for example, seven hundred New Yorkers attended a birthday ball in Paine's honor. Labor unions and workingmen's political parties held Paine birthday dinners where speakers toasted *The Age of Reason* as "a work containing more truth than any volume under the sun."

Why did Paine become such a hero to workers years after his death? Part of the answer can be found in the personality and experiences of the man himself. He was one of the few leading figures of the American Revolution to know real poverty during periods of his life. At a time when most writers used elaborate figures of speech and Latin phrases to impress well-educated readers, Paine aimed for "language as plain as the alphabet" to "make those that can scarcely read understand." Paine had also called for a tax on wealthy landlords to provide a public fund for improving the lot of ordinary tenants and landless people. His Deism made sense to some working people who, rather than seeing Christian clergymen as friends of the poor, regarded them as the allies of wealthy merchants and manufacturers.

It was the overall message of Paine's life and work that really made him a working-class hero. Paine's American Revolution was a struggle fought as much for the rights of the artisan and farmer as for the wealthy merchant or lawyer. More than that, Paine realized that it was a struggle fought *by* such common people. The moral of Paine's own life was that a poor and obscure immigrant staymaker could challenge the vast power of the British monarchy, the French monarchy, and organized Christianity. American radicals in the Jacksonian era learned their own lesson from Paine's Revolution: Common men and women could reshape their world if they had the courage to challenge the authority of the rich and powerful.

This Fourth of July Is Yours, Not Mine

ABOLITIONISTS, FEMINISTS, AND THE CIVIL WAR

☞ *The Book of Fate*

In March 1775, one month before the Revolutionary War broke out at Lexington and Concord, Thomas Paine asked his fellow Americans an embarrassing and painful question: How could they dare to "complain so loudly of attempts to enslave them, while they hold so many hundred thousand in slavery"?

Throughout America, African-Americans lived and worked as slaves on plantations, on farms, and in towns. By the eve of the Revolution in 1775, about a half million black people (one out of every five Americans) were slaves.

Although most labored for white masters all their lives without any hope of gaining freedom, slaves managed to hold on to many of the things that make life meaningful to all human beings. They maintained their own family life, and they preserved customs and beliefs that they had brought with them from Africa. But they also adapted those customs to New World surroundings, creating a unique culture that was both African and American. Slaves could never forget that they were forced to work without pay, that they could be whipped or beaten by their owners, and could be sold away from loved ones, never to see them again. Yet in their religion, music, work, and play, slaves found renewal and forged a way of life that shaped even the world of their white masters.

Before the American Revolution, most white colonists accepted slavery as a natural part of their society. But the struggle for liberty against British oppression forced many to confront the injustice of slavery. Paine's unanswered question would not go away: If all human beings were entitled to live in freedom, how could whites hold blacks in bondage?

In the years after the War for Independence, state after state in the North, where slavery was not so important economically, abolished it. Revolutionary leaders such as Alexander Hamilton, John Jay, and Benjamin Franklin helped spearhead the antislavery drive in New York and Pennsylvania.

Even in the South, where white owners of tobacco, rice, and indigo plantations lived off the wealth produced by their slave workers, the Founding Fathers were troubled by the reality of human bondage. Some freed their slaves. Among them was George Washington, who made sure in his will that, after the death of his widow Martha, the remaining slaves at Mount Vernon would be given their freedom.

Another Virginian, Thomas Jefferson, had more complicated feelings about slavery. On one hand, Jefferson suspected that blacks were naturally inferior to whites in terms of their intellectual ability. He also feared that if all slaves were freed in the South, a bloody race war might break out as angry blacks sought vengeance against their former masters. The only possible way of preventing this would be to remove freed slaves from America and make them settle in some other part of the world where they would not be a threat to whites.

On the other hand, Jefferson hated slavery. He saw it as a form of tyranny—a tyranny like that which George III tried to impose on the colonies. He even attempted to put a condemnation of the slave trade in the Declaration of Independence, but other congressional delegates from the South vetoed it. Emancipation of the slaves, he believed, was coming. "Nothing is more certainly written in the book of fate," he asserted, "than that these people are to be free." Jefferson used his political influence to stop slavery from spreading into newly settled parts of the western frontier. He helped, for example, to shape the Northwest Ordinance of 1787, which kept slavery out of the territories of Ohio, Indiana, Illinois, Michigan, and Wisconsin.

Jefferson was also willing to admit that he might be wrong to think that

As his slaves work, George Washington strolls through Mount Vernon's fields with his stepchildren, Jackie and Patsy, in this print published two years before the start of the Civil War. Courtesy of the New York Public Library.

whites were intellectually superior to blacks. Since slaves were not allowed an education, and since whites automatically assumed that blacks were inferior, Jefferson realized that it was all too easy for white observers like himself to misjudge the abilities of slaves. He applauded when African-Americans like the free mathematician Benjamin Banneker provided evidence of exceptional intelligence and talent.

"Whatever be their degree of talent," he wrote of black Americans, "it is no measure of their rights." What really mattered to Jefferson was that all men—black and white, regardless of ability—should be able to enjoy life, liberty, and the pursuit of happiness. To be able to share freedom equally: This was what

Jefferson had meant when he asserted that "All men are created equal" in the Declaration of Independence.

Yet Jefferson himself was a slaveholder. The day-to-day work on his estate at Monticello—the farming, the cooking, the household cleaning—was performed not by Thomas Jefferson, but by his human property. Whatever guilt he may have felt, Jefferson never freed his slaves, even when his political enemies spread rumors about his relationship with Sally Hemings. This was because Jefferson was unable to free himself from his lifelong dependence on slavery. Jefferson's whole way of life, like that of many white Southerners, was built on slave labor. It was the income from his plantation crops, grown and harvested by his slaves, that allowed him to devote his energies to the cause of the American Revolution. Despite his passion for the idea of liberty, he was never able to find his own personal solution to the ugly reality of slavery.

☞ Patriots of the Second Revolution

By the time of Jefferson's death in 1826, fewer and fewer voices in the South dared to question slavery as Jefferson had. In 1793 a young Northerner named Eli Whitney had invented a machine, the cotton gin, that made it easy and profitable to prepare the fibers of the cotton plant for sale to textile manufacturers. Cotton plantations spread throughout the South, and whites bought slaves to plant and pick the crop. As they made money from cotton, white Southerners grew more and more committed to what they now called their "peculiar institution" of slavery.

They were opposed by the abolitionists, a small but vocal group of white and black Northerners. Though slavery had already been abolished in the North, the abolitionists were not satisfied. They would accept nothing less than the complete elimination of the evil of slavery from the United States. Abolitionists wanted to create an America where free blacks and whites could live in harmony; they rejected the approach of other antislavery activists, known as colonizationists, who fulfilled Jefferson's vision by sending free blacks out of the country to a settlement in West Africa called Liberia.

Some abolitionists were angry at the Founding Fathers for not going far

enough to destroy American slavery. Because Washington, Hamilton, and the other framers of the Constitution had not outlawed slavery in the Southern states, the abolitionist William Lloyd Garrison denounced the document as "an agreement with Hell" and publicly burned a copy of it in protest. And even though George Washington had eventually freed his slaves, the fact that he lived off their labor during his own lifetime bothered antislavery activists. Visiting Mount Vernon, Susan B. Anthony was upset by the thought that it was here "that he whose name is the pride of the nation was the *Slave Master.*"

Another Northerner, James T. Woodbury, was actually converted to the abolitionist cause by a visit to Washington's grave at Mount Vernon. His guide to the tomb was an elderly former slave of Washington's. When asked about his children, the old man replied: "I don't know whether they are alive or dead. They were all sold away from me, and I don't know what became of them. I am alone in the world, without a child to bring me a cup of water in my old age." Woodbury reached his own conclusion: "This is the fate of slaves, even when owned by so good a man as General Washington! Who would not be an Abolitionist?"

Other abolitionists, however, embraced the Founding Fathers for helping to begin the movement against slavery. Even though Jefferson, Franklin, and Hamilton had not ended slavery in the United States, the fact that they all denounced it meant that slavery was "un-American." The abolitionist Wendell Phillips accused slavery's defenders of violating the revolutionary "Spirit of 1776."

In Boston, an African-American abolitionist went even further. William Cooper Nell had been born to free parents in Massachusetts in 1816. An honors student in school, he had watched in humiliation as white students received prizes while he was denied an award simply because of his skin color. His anger at racial inequality convinced him to devote his life to the abolitionist cause. As a young man, he launched a fifteen-year campaign to end racial segregation in the Boston public school system. He finally won the battle in 1855.

That same year, Nell wrote and published a book entitled *The Colored*

Patriots of the American Revolution. He based his book on careful historical research and interviews. Nell discovered that Americans had forgotten a whole group of heroes who had risked their lives for liberty: the black soldiers of the Revolution. Five thousand African-Americans had fought on the patriot side during the war. Some fought as freemen; others were promised and given their freedom by grateful masters and state governments.

Nell did not try to conceal the fact that some blacks had also fought for the enemy side. The British had offered freedom to those slaves who would run away from their American masters and help to put down the colonists' rebellion. Gaining their freedom was so precious to slaves, Nell pointed out, that it was not surprising that some fought *against* American independence to win their own liberty.

The real heroes of Nell's book were the men who fought against the redcoats, and he told the stories of dozens of black revolutionaries. Peter Salem, for example, helped at the Battle of Bunker Hill by shooting a British officer as he tried to rally his troops. Oliver Cromwell had served in the Second New Jersey Regiment, and fought in most of the important battles in his native state. At the age of one hundred, in 1852, he still remembered having "knocked the British about lively" at the Battle of Princeton. In some of the bloodiest fighting of the war, a regiment of four hundred black soldiers from Rhode Island beat back an attack by Hessians at the Battle of Red Bank. Nell's book contained many more examples of black patriots who had fought and died for American independence.

For Nell, the most important of these heroes was Crispus Attucks. In his own day, and in Nell's era eighty-five years later, Attucks was a mysterious figure. Most details of his life went unrecorded. He seems to have been born a slave in Massachusetts, and may have been part Indian. Attucks ran away from his master as a young man and, like many other black men, sought his freedom as a sailor on whaling vessels.

Attucks would have remained unknown if not for the events that were building to a climax in the city of Boston in early March 1770. For several months, British troops had been stationed in the town to maintain control

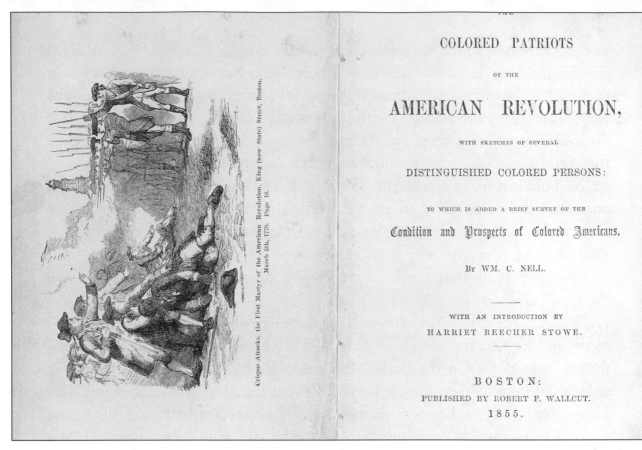

COLORED PATRIOTS

OF THE

AMERICAN REVOLUTION,

WITH SKETCHES OF SEVERAL

DISTINGUISHED COLORED PERSONS:

TO WHICH IS ADDED A BRIEF SURVEY OF THE

Condition and Prospects of Colored Americans.

By WM. C. NELL.

WITH AN INTRODUCTION BY
HARRIET BEECHER STOWE.

BOSTON:
PUBLISHED BY ROBERT F. WALLCUT.
1855.

While earlier depictions of the Boston Massacre (including one drawn by Paul Revere) left out Crispus Attucks, William C. Nell made sure his book featured a picture of the black "martyr of the Revolution." Courtesy of the Library of Congress, Rare Book and Special Collections Division, LC-USZ 62-55356.

over colonists who openly boycotted English goods and challenged the right of Parliament to levy taxes. Not only were Bostonians insulted to be treated like "desperadoes" by the English authorities, many were enraged by the fact that off-duty redcoats took part-time jobs in local businesses. In the eyes of Bostonians who labored on the port's docks and in its workshops, English troops were stealing their jobs as well as threatening their liberties.

On the cold moonlit night of March 5, Crispus Attucks was one of the leaders of a crowd of angry men and boys who marched up King Street to confront the small detachment of English soldiers standing guard at the Boston customhouse. Shouts and curses flew back and forth, and the colonists started

★ THIS FOURTH OF JULY IS *YOURS*, NOT *MINE*

hurling snowballs and rocks at the soldiers. Attucks stepped forward and grabbed the bayonet of a panicking Englishman. A volley of shots rang out, and eleven of the Americans fell to the snow-covered ground. Attucks lay dying with two musket balls lodged in his chest.

The "Boston Massacre" became a rallying point for Americans outraged by the actions of their so-called mother country. Although five more years would pass before the colonists began their War for Independence, the shooting pushed Americans further along the road to rebellion. Many considered Attucks and the four other Bostonians who died to be the first martyrs of the revolutionary movement.

On March 5, 1851, Nell and six other free African-Americans presented a petition to the Massachusetts legislature. In it they asked that money be appropriated to erect a monument in Boston to Crispus Attucks. The legislature turned them down. But Nell and other Boston abolitionists continued to press for public recognition of Attucks's importance. In 1858 they began to celebrate March 5 every year as Crispus Attucks Day.

In doing so, they gave black Americans their own national holiday. Because millions of slaves remained unfree in the South, many free blacks in the North refused to celebrate Independence Day on July 4. "This Fourth [of] July is *yours,* not *mine,*" the black abolitionist Frederick Douglass told white audiences. "*You* may rejoice, *I* must mourn." Instead, Nell and his comrades encouraged blacks to celebrate their own Founding Father, who had died a free man fighting for American rights.

By demanding public recognition of Attucks's sacrifice, Nell was trying to remind all Americans that blacks had played a meaningful role in winning the nation's independence. Many whites in the North as well as in the South wanted to forget that.

Some Northern whites actively collaborated in helping the South keep its slaves. The Fugitive Slave Law, passed by Congress in 1850, required Northerners to return runaway slaves to their Southern owners. In Boston, federal agents captured a fugitive slave named Anthony Burns and prepared to return him to his master in Virginia.

Abolitionists resisted the law. They raided the courthouse where Burns was imprisoned, but failed to free him. To prevent his escape, one thousand United States soldiers escorted Burns through the Boston streets, down to the docks where he was put on a ship for the journey back to bondage. In Nell's words, Burns was "dragged back to slavery . . . marching over the very ground that ATTUCKS trod." Keeping the memory of Attucks alive was a way of hammering home the shame and horror of American slavery.

Despite the Fugitive Slave Law, Nell was optimistic that the grandsons and granddaughters of the revolutionaries would match the courage and self-sacrifice of their forefathers. Nell noted proudly that free black men in New York City and Cincinnati were forming their own militia companies called the Attucks Guards. Like the workers who had made Thomas Paine a hero because they saw him as symbolizing their own struggle for equality, Nell had looked back to the Revolution and found black patriots whose deeds could inspire his own generation of African-Americans to persist in their fight for the rights set forth in the Declaration of Independence. The time for submitting to the demands of Southern slavemasters and Northern racists, Nell predicted, was drawing to a close. A new revolutionary struggle was coming, one that would be fought for the cause of universal brotherhood. William Nell eagerly awaited the heroic deeds to be done by the black "Patriots of the Second Revolution."

☞ *All Men and Women Are Created Equal*

In 1840 Lucretia Mott, Elizabeth Cady Stanton, and other female American abolitionists attended a World Anti-Slavery Convention in London, England. Mott and the others had devoted their lives to the fight against slavery. As organizers, writers, and speechmakers, they had proved themselves to be as brave and effective as their male counterparts. To their outrage and disgust, the men who controlled the London Convention refused to let them participate actively. Women were permitted to remain in the hall only if they consented to sit behind a curtain, removed from public view.

These women had already encountered such discrimination in America.

When female abolitionist orators tried to speak to mixed audiences of men and women, many objected that it was wrong for women to address men. Men were supposed to lecture women, not the other way around. There were limits, such critics said, to the role women could properly play in public affairs. Females should leave the management of reform and political activities to men, who were "naturally" endowed with the intelligence and aggressiveness needed for public life. Women who stepped out of the "modest" role expected of them were acting in an "unwomanly" and "unnatural" way. In 1840 the heated debate over the "woman question" divided the abolitionist movement into two factions, one favoring female equality, the other hostile to it.

Mott and Stanton knew all too well that the animosity of some of their male abolitionist colleagues was only part of a larger problem. Throughout American society, men treated women as inferior beings. Most colleges refused to take female students. Laws kept women from voting or running for office. When women married, their husbands were automatically entitled to take over their property. Poor women labored in factories or as domestic servants for lower wages than men received for the same work. On the other hand, middle-class and wealthy women were not supposed to have careers at all, but were expected to stay at home and let their husbands be the family breadwinners. Politicians, teachers, clergymen, and writers all told women that their natural "delicacy" and "spirituality" suited them for lives as wives and mothers, while they lacked the intelligence and strength that men possessed for involvement in the public world of business and politics.

Mott and Stanton knew this was wrong. They had learned it in their own busy public lives as abolitionist crusaders. Slowly but surely, they and other feminists began to compare the position of American women with that of black slaves. "True," one feminist admitted, "we have not felt the slave-holder's lash; true, we have not had our hands manacled, but our *hearts* have been crushed."

In July 1848 Mott, Stanton, and other female reformers organized their own meeting in the village of Seneca Falls, New York. About two hundred delegates, including thirty-two men, attended the world's first Women's Rights

Convention, braving the taunts of mainstream newspapers and speechmakers who ridiculed them as "mannish" women and "Aunt Nancy Men."

The Founding Fathers were very much on the minds of the convention delegates. Once more, the revolutionary leaders of 1776 had let them down. Just as Jefferson and his colleagues had failed to eliminate slavery from the land, they had also failed to create a nation that granted equality to American women.

The attitude of the Founders toward women, Stanton later suggested, was revealed by the way some of them treated the females in their own lives. During the eleven years that Benjamin Franklin lived in Europe, he was heartless enough to leave his wife Deborah at home alone in Philadelphia to raise their children. Deborah died while her husband was in England. "Undazzled by the glories of Franklin stoves and lightning rods," Stanton charged, "one sees much to disapprove in the life of the great philosopher!!" If one of the greatest of all Americans treated women so poorly, Stanton implied, was it any wonder that most American men regarded women as inferior?

Yet the Founders had also given the world the Declaration of Independence, and the women's rights activists found a way to take the achievement of Jefferson a step further. For the Seneca Falls Convention, Stanton drafted a Declaration of Sentiments and Resolutions that was modeled word for word on Jefferson's Declaration. But Stanton changed a few things. *Her* version declared, "We hold these truths to be self-evident: that all men and women are created equal." Where Jefferson had listed the acts of injustice ordered by George III against the colonies, Stanton provided examples of the "absolute tyranny" that men tried to establish over women. After listing the ways in which the American man deprived the American woman of her political, educational, and economic rights, Stanton noted that "He has endeavored, in every way that he could, to destroy her confidence in her own powers, to lessen her self-respect, and to make her willing to lead a dependent and abject life."

To restore women to the enjoyment of their equal rights, Stanton offered the delegates a series of resolutions. All but one of the resolutions passed easily when the delegates voted on them. The assembled reformers had no problem with the measures condemning all laws that discriminated against women, or that called for the right of women to speak, teach, and write in public on the pressing issues of the day. But it took the eloquence of the African-American leader Frederick Douglass, one of the thirty-two male delegates, to convince the others to pass Stanton's resolution advocating the right of women to vote, and then only by a narrow majority. That measure seemed almost too daring, too radical, even for the reformers gathered at Seneca Falls.

☞ *The Women of the American Revolution*

It would take over seventy years of struggle by feminists for American women to win the right to vote through an amendment to the Constitution in 1920. During those years, feminists tried to convince others that women had proven their equality throughout American history. The Revolution provided them with some of their most effective examples.

One piece of evidence they could use was a book, first published in 1848, by a writer named Elizabeth Ellet. Her work was entitled *The Women of the American Revolution*. As a little girl in upstate New York, Ellet had first become interested in history when she heard tales about her grandfather, who had fought as a captain in the Revolutionary War. Like William C. Nell, Ellet wanted to revive memories of a forgotten group of revolutionaries.

Ellet herself was not a feminist; her goal was not to win political or civil rights for women. But she felt the need to do justice to those women who had played a part in the revolutionary struggle. The standard history books said little or nothing about the contribution of women to the cause of independence. Ellet was determined to tell their stories. She tracked down old diaries and letters hidden away in family scrapbooks, and she interviewed elderly people who still remembered the events of the Revolution. Ellet recovered the stories of so many female patriots that the first edition of her book had to be published in two volumes. *The Women of the American Revolution* went through several editions, and was still being published in the twentieth century.

Ellet discovered that women had helped the revolutionary movement in a surprising variety of ways. Throughout the thirteen colonies, housewives boycotted British tea and other imports. Rather than buy English textiles, they wove their own cloth and made their own clothing. Once the war started, women also played crucial roles. They organized drives in their villages and towns to raise money for the Continental Army. Because British officers rarely took the political and military interests of women seriously, females made excellent spies and messengers behind enemy lines. While their men were off fighting the redcoats, wives and daughters ran family farms and businesses. By doing so, they helped to keep the American economy going and fed the troops.

All ranks of women contributed, and a select few even influenced the men who ran the new nation. Mercy Warren, for example, was the sister of lawyer James Otis and the wife of James Warren, both prominent Boston patriots. In a society that frowned on the idea of higher education for women, Warren managed to attain an impressive knowledge of history, literature, and politics by teaching herself. Because of her husband's involvement in the revolutionary cause, Warren knew Samuel Adams, John Adams, Thomas Jefferson, and other Founding Fathers, all of whom recognized her brilliance. As Ellet put it, "these men asked her opinion in political matters, and acknowledged the excellence of her judgment." After the war, Warren wrote a history of the Revolution, making her the first serious female historian in America.

Others became revolutionaries in more active ways. In order to be close to their husbands and fathers, the families of many revolutionary soldiers followed the troops in their movements through the thirteen states. The wives of soldiers performed traditional duties by cooking and cleaning for their men. But in the heat of battle, some proved their courage and skill as soldiers. When her husband, an artilleryman, was killed during a British attack on Fort Washington in New York, Margaret Cochran took his place at the cannon and was wounded herself. After the war, Congress awarded her a military pension in thanks for her service. Mary McCauley, who became known as "Molly

Mercy Otis Warren, patriot and historian, painted by John Singleton Copley in 1763.
Courtesy of the Museum of Fine Arts, Boston. Bequest of Winslow Warren.

Pitcher" for similar coolness under fire at the Battle of Monmouth, also received a government reward in later years.

But the most dramatic and unusual case of wartime bravery was that of Deborah Sampson. Sampson's story had become legendary by the 1840s, but Ellet attempted to sort out the facts of her life. Sampson was born in 1760 in Massachusetts, where her father, who had trouble making a living out of his small farm and who drank too much, abandoned his family and disappeared. As a child, Deborah was "bound out" as a servant to another family. She possessed a "mind naturally superior," and like Mercy Warren, she insisted on getting as much education as she could. At age eighteen, she enrolled herself as a pupil in the local schoolhouse, and excelled as a student. The growing struggle over colonial rights aroused Sampson's patriotism. She "bitterly regretted . . . that she had not the privilege of a man, of shedding her blood for her country."

But in 1782 she found a way around this problem. Leaving her job as a village schoolteacher, she went into the woods carrying a bundle of men's clothing. She reemerged with a new identity. As "Robert Shirtliffe," she enlisted in the Fourth Massachusetts Regiment of the American army. Sampson was able to conceal her identity through an entire year of wartime service. During that time, "Shirtliffe" took part in several engagements with the enemy, and was

This woodcut, printed in Massachusetts during the Revolution, captures the dedication of women like Margaret Cochran and Deborah Sampson, who shouldered arms to fight the redcoats. From "A New Touch on the Times . . . By a Daughter of Liberty, living in Marblehead," 1779. Courtesy of the collection of the New-York Historical Society.

wounded during a skirmish with British troops near Tarrytown, New York. It was only after "he" was hospitalized for fever that a doctor discovered the soldier's secret. Following the discovery, General Henry Knox gave Sampson an honorable discharge from the army in October 1783.

After the war, Sampson returned to the Massachusetts countryside, married a farmer named Benjamin Gannett, and raised three children. But the stories of her wartime exploits circulated widely. In 1802 a writer named Herman Mann persuaded Sampson to tour New England and New York, delivering an "Address" written by Mann before audiences of paying theatergoers. Adults paid twenty-five cents, children half price to hear "Mrs. Gannet, the celebrated American Heroine." Many came expecting to see a hoax. Sampson noted in her diary that she overheard some in the audience who "swore that I was a lad of not more than eighteen years of age." Dressed in full military uniform, Sampson took the stage and admitted that she had been "unnatural, unwise and indelicate" in leaving the "paths of female delicacy" to play a man's part in the Revolution. But her patriotism and anger at redcoat cruelty, she claimed, got the better of her judgment. Recalling her skirmish, Sampson told her audience, "I was there! The recollection makes me shudder!—A dislocated limb draws fresh anguish from my heart!" After finishing a performance, Sampson noted that the audience had given her its "serious attention and peculiar respect, especially the ladies."

Whether or not Sampson really agreed with the apology for her "unfeminine" behavior that Herman Mann wrote for her, the tour was a success. Sampson made money from it, and the address stirred up publicity that helped her to win a government pension in 1805 for her wartime service; another veteran of the Revolution, Paul Revere, helped her to get the money by writing to Congress.

Sampson actually broke two stereotypes of female behavior. Not only had she proved her ability as a soldier, but she was one of the first American women to become a public lecturer. Sampson's brief military career put her way ahead of her time. But her accomplishments, like those of Mercy Warren, also made assumptions of female inferiority seem unjust and inaccurate.

Didn't Deborah Sampson's success as a soldier suggest that women possessed abilities that were wasted if they were confined to the kitchen and nursery? Forced to confront the life story of Mercy Warren, how could American men argue that women were intellectually inferior, and deny them equal access to higher education? Words written by a Bostonian named Hannah Winthrop in the revolutionary 1770s and published by Elizabeth Ellet in 1848 could only boost the morale of feminists as they fought to win the vote for American women: "Be it known unto Britain, even American daughters are politicians and patriots, and will aid the good work with their female efforts."

☞ *The Declaration of Independence Includes All Men*

While feminists organized to denounce and fight sexual discrimination, the dispute between Northerners and Southerners over slavery was building toward an angry and violent confrontation. By the 1830s and 1840s, Southern slaveowners had come to feel that their way of life separated them from the rest of the country. They were furious at the antislavery activities of Northern abolitionists. Increasingly, Southerners argued that the citizens of the North and South were really two separate peoples who could share one government only if Northerners stopped trying to interfere with Southern slavery. Many Southerners also demanded the right to take their slaves into United States territories on the western frontier, where they intended to set up new slave states.

Whites in the South expressed these feelings by taking pride in all things Southern. Naturally, they turned to the American Revolution for proof of Southern courage and leadership. After all, two of the greatest Americans of all time—George Washington and Thomas Jefferson—had been Virginians and Southerners. Unlike abolitionists, Southern slavemasters took pride in the fact that Washington and Jefferson had owned human property. As John C. Calhoun of South Carolina argued, Washington "was one of us—a slaveholder and a planter."

Southerners like Calhoun sent a defiant message to the North: America's greatest men had owned slaves, and Southerners had no intention of freeing their slaves now. As Georgia Senator Robert Toombs declared in 1856, Jefferson "owned slaves. . . . He kept them as long as he lived; he consumed their labor without wages. . . . This is the model held up to the American people."

Such statements angered Northerners, who were coming to resent Southerners just as much as Southerners resented them. By the 1850s the cause of antislavery was no longer limited to a small group of abolitionist "fanatics." White Northerners in growing numbers now saw Southern politicians and slaveowners as power-hungry men who not only wanted to preserve slavery in their own states, but to spread its evil throughout the rest of American society.

In 1854 Northerners formed a new political party, the Republicans, in order to fight Southern attempts to spread slavery into the western territories. One Republican leader, an Illinois lawyer and politician named Abraham Lincoln, challenged the Southern argument that the Founding Fathers had been pro-slavery. As a boy living on frontier farms in Kentucky and Indiana, Lincoln's imagination had been filled with the battles of the Revolution. He later remembered that "away back in my childhood, the earliest days of my being able to read, I got hold of a small book, . . . 'Weems' Life of Washington.' " He remembered thinking as a boy that "there must have been something more than common that those men struggled for."

As an adult, Lincoln maintained that Washington, Jefferson, and other Founders had tried to keep slavery from spreading beyond the borders of the states where it already existed. Alexander Hamilton, Benjamin Franklin, and New York revolutionary Gouverneur Morris had been among "the most noted anti-slavery men of those times." As he ran for the presidency in 1860, Lincoln told Americans that they should continue to view slavery as the Founders had: "as an evil not to be extended" into western territories, "but to be tolerated and protected" only in those Southern states where it was already established.

Again and again, Lincoln challenged the Southern view of Thomas Jefferson as a man who accepted and approved of slavery. Nothing could be further from the truth, he argued. The fact that Jefferson owned slaves was far less important than the document he had given to the world in July 1776. "The Declaration of Independence includes ALL men, black as well as white," Lincoln stated, and its guarantees of life, liberty, and the pursuit of happiness meant that "*all* should have an equal chance."

But Lincoln also warned that "it is now no child's play to save the principles of Jefferson from total overthrow in this nation." His warning seemed to come true after his election to the presidency in November 1860. One by one, the Southern states seceded from the Union, convinced that they could no longer be part of the United States under a president who opposed the expansion of slavery.

In February 1861 seven Southern states (South Carolina, Mississippi, Florida, Alabama, Georgia, Louisiana, and Texas) formed a new nation, the Confederate States of America, dedicated to the preservation of slavery. They were later joined by Arkansas, North Carolina, Virginia, and Tennessee. Lincoln refused to accept the Confederacy, and argued that states had no right under the Constitution to secede from the United States. When, in April 1861, Union troops following Lincoln's orders refused to evacuate Fort Sumter in the harbor of Charleston, South Carolina, Confederate gunners opened fire. The Civil War, the bloodiest conflict in American history, had begun.

"The Confederate States of 1861 are acting over again the history of the American Revolution of 1776," a Southern newspaper declared on the first Fourth of July during the war. White Southerners were fighting to preserve the independence of their new nation, and to defend their way of life. It was easy for Southerners to see themselves as fighting the second American Revolution, except this time the enemy was the North, not Great Britain. After all, weren't they going into battle to defend their liberties, which included their right to own slaves? Wasn't President Lincoln acting the tyrant by asking his Congress to mobilize Northern troops to crush the Confederacy?

By seceding from the Union to protect "Liberty and Equality for white men," Southerners maintained, the Southern states were merely doing what Jefferson would have wanted them to do if he were still alive. Jefferson had always been a passionate defender of the rights of the individual states, espe-

Bunker Hill, symbolizing the "spirit of 1776," looms on the horizon as Union troops rally in this tableau painted by a Northerner during the Civil War. Courtesy of the New York State Historical Association, Cooperstown, New York.

cially when those states found themselves at the mercy of a powerful and overbearing federal government. He felt that the state governments should protect and preserve the liberties of the people if the federal government ever acted in a tyrannical way.

Lincoln and many Northerners rejected this argument. In their view, the Constitution did not give any state the right to separate itself from the Union. The Founding Fathers had created a unified nation, not a mere collection of independent states. The way to preserve and strengthen the principles of life, liberty, and the pursuit of happiness that Jefferson himself had fought for was to preserve the Union. This meant raising an army to crush the Southern rebels, and to bring the Southern states back into the United States. As one Lincoln supporter put it, "If it was worth a bloody struggle to establish this nation, it is worth one to preserve it."

Once the war was underway and young Northerners and Southerners were fighting and dying on the battlefield, both sides continued to claim the Revolutionary Founders as their own. George Washington in particular was present everywhere in both the North and the South during the war. His face appeared on paper money and postage stamps; his memory was celebrated in songs and poems; and Jefferson Davis, the president of the Confederacy, was sworn into office on Washington's Birthday under a statue of the Founding Father. About the only thing that the Union and Confederate armies agreed on was that Washington's estate at Mount Vernon should be neutral ground, undisturbed by war.

But the memory of Washington meant very different things to "Yankees" and "Rebs." Northerners celebrated Washington as the general who had protected the fledgling United States by defeating the British, the statesman who had helped create a stronger Union by presiding over the Constitutional Convention, and the president who had limited the westward spread of slavery by endorsing the Northwest Ordinance. To Southerners, Washington was simply the greatest Virginian and slaveowner who had ever lived. He had led a rebel army to victory against the numerically superior troops of a tyrannical Britain, in much the same way that the Confederate army was trying to hold its own against the more numerous and better-supplied troops of Lincoln's Union regiments.

The Confederacy's leading general, Robert E. Lee, idolized Washington. His father, "Light-Horse Harry" Lee, had been a Revolutionary War hero and a friend of the first president. This only increased the conviction of Southerners that Washington was "theirs" and not to be shared with Northerners.

Soldiers on both sides sought inspiration and courage from the examples of other heroes. Especially dear to Southern troops was the memory of Francis Marion, the legendary "Swamp Fox" of the Revolution. Marion had conducted a brilliant hit-and-run campaign against the British in South Carolina; his troops would seemingly appear out of nowhere to attack redcoat supply lines and Tory outposts, only to disappear back into the state's forbidding swamps and marshlands. Confederate cavalrymen rode into battle singing verses from "The Song of Marion's Men":

> *Our band is few, but true and tried,*
> *Our leader frank and bold;*
> *The British soldier trembles*
> *When Marion's name is told.*

The horsemen did not pause to remember that the song had actually been written before the Civil War by a Northerner, the antislavery poet William Cullen Bryant.

Northern soldiers had their own heroes. Black troops fighting for the Union, for example, remembered the African-American patriots of the Revolution. Especially after President Lincoln issued the Emancipation Proclamation, free black men flocked into newly formed "colored" regiments. Eventually 180,000 black soldiers and sailors served in the Union forces, and Lincoln credited them with helping to win the war for the North. A soldier of Company A of the Massachusetts 54th Regiment, the first all-black regiment to prove itself in battle against Confederate troops in Marion's state of South Carolina, wrote a song to be shared by all African-Americans serving in the Union armies and navies. In it he reminded his fellow volunteers of their ancestors who had fought to uphold the stars and stripes in the Revolutionary War and the War of 1812:

> *Oh, give us a flag, all free without a slave*
> *We'll fight to defend it as our fathers did so brave*
> *The gallant Comp'ny 'A' will make the Rebels dance*
> *And we'll stand by the Union if we only have a chance.*

Francis Marion (center), the South Carolina "Swamp Fox," became a Southern hero during the Civil War. In this nineteenth-century picture by John Blake White, a slave (left) serves the revolutionary general.

On April 9, 1865, after four long years of war, Robert E. Lee surrendered his exhausted Confederate army to the Union forces of General Ulysses S. Grant at Appomattox Courthouse in Virginia. The Civil War, which had taken six hundred thousand lives, was over. Slavery was dead forever, and the defeated Confederacy lay in ruins. With peace, Americans Northern and Southern, black and white, began the difficult process of putting their lives in order.

On the evening of April 14, while attending a play at Ford's Theatre in Washington, President Lincoln was shot in the head and killed by John Wilkes Booth, a Southern sympathizer. The news of the assassination plunged the people of the North into shock and grief. The man who had held the Union together and freed the slaves was dead.

During his presidency, Lincoln had many supporters in the North, but he also had his critics. Some argued that he did not possess the vision or strength of character to guide the Union through its most severe crisis since the Revolution. The Northern writer Francis Parkman complained during the war that "an endangered nation seeks a leader worthy of itself. . . . Out of three millions, America found a Washington, an Adams, a Franklin, a Jefferson, a Hamilton; out of twenty millions, she now finds none whose stature can compare with these."

But after Lincoln's assassination, the grieving people of the North joined together almost unanimously to praise his greatness. Old criticisms were forgotten; the traits for which Lincoln had been noted in his lifetime—his honesty, his plain speaking, his ordinariness—were elevated into almost godlike qualities by poets, newspaper writers, and artists.

Americans paid Lincoln the highest compliment by comparing him with the man they still considered to be the greatest statesman in their history, George Washington. Like Washington, Northerners argued, Lincoln had led his people through war and chaos to victory and peace; the honesty and decency of both men in private life matched their greatness in public life. One poet pictured the moment when Lincoln entered Heaven:

> *Heroes and Saints with fadeless stars have crowned him—and*
> *WASHINGTON's dear arms are clasped around him.*

By putting Lincoln and Washington together in their own minds, Northerners after the Civil War showed just how important Washington and the other Founding Fathers remained to them. Almost one hundred years after the Revolution, Americans were still measuring their leaders against the heroes of that earlier struggle. The principles of liberty, equality, and independence that nineteenth-century Americans held with such fierce pride, and that many of them still struggled to obtain in their own lives, were tied to the Revolution. As the fight for women's rights began and Southern slavery became the most controversial issue in American politics, different Americans interpreted the meanings of liberty, equality, and independence in different ways, and chose different heroes for themselves. But one thing, at least, connected the abolitionists who discovered their own Founding Father in Crispus Attucks, the feminists who rewrote Jefferson's Declaration of Independence, and the Confederate soldiers who sang songs about Francis Marion: They all looked back to the Revolution in order to come to grips with their *own* America, and to help them in their efforts to shape their country's uncertain future.

George Washington welcomes the assassinated Abraham Lincoln into heaven, 1865. Courtesy of Lloyd Ostendorf.

The Disease of Democracy
BUSINESSMEN, NATIVE AMERICANS, AND POPULISTS

☞*America at One Hundred*

On May 10, 1876, thousands of sightseers poured through the gates of Philadelphia's Fairmount Park to begin celebrating the hundredth birthday of the United States of America. They were heading for the Centennial Exposition, a 450-acre fairground created to show what Americans had accomplished in their first century of independence. After paying their fifty cents' admission and entering the Exposition grounds, visitors fanned out to explore the acre upon acre of special exhibits designed to impress and delight them. They admired statues of Christopher Columbus and Elias Howe (inventor of the sewing machine), and bought refreshments at the soda-water fountains and cigar pavilions scattered throughout the park. To get from one attraction to another, many chose to spend an extra five cents for a ride on the Exposition's steam railroad, or for sixty cents an hour hired attendants to push them around in specially built "rolling chairs." Most took time to inspect the Exposition's Main Hall, a vast structure of glass supported by iron columns and girders, at two and a half acres, the largest building in the world.

But the biggest attraction was Machinery Hall. Here visitors inspected a wide range of new contraptions invented by Americans: Thomas Edison's multiple-message telegraph, the Remington typewriter, and a strange device called the telephone, concocted by one Alexander Graham Bell. Most impressive of all was the seven-hundred-ton, forty-foot-high steam-powered Double Walking-Beam Engine, invented by George H. Corliss of Rhode Island. A huge monster of a machine, the engine generated enough power to run all the other machinery in the hall. From opening day, the engine and the Exposition's hundreds of other displays were a smashing success. By the time it closed six months later, almost ten million people had visited the Centennial Exposition.

As Americans celebrated the hundredth anniversary of their independence that summer of 1876, many felt proud of their achievements. Industrialists, merchants, bankers, and other businessmen who had invested money to build factories, railroads, and mines were especially pleased. In one century, they and their predecessors had turned a country of farmers and shopkeepers into one of the world's major industrial powers. Railroads now crossed the continent, linking the East to the West Coast, increasing the sense of a unified nation. The Corliss Engine, Edison's and Bell's inventions, and the steam railway proved the ingenuity and enterprise of American manufacturers and inventors. Now that their terrible Civil War was behind them, many hoped that all Americans, both Northern and Southern, would work together to show the world what a free and industrious people could achieve.

Yet others viewed centennial America as a land of shattered hopes. As throngs of Exposition tourists peered at tepees and arrowheads put on display by curators from the Smithsonian Institution, the Plains tribes were preparing to fight the last desperate battles to keep their land from encroaching settlers. Tools and produce in Agricultural Hall showcased the glories of American farming. But thousands of farm families felt victimized by high warehouse and railway rates charged by the very businessmen taking credit for American progress. Indeed, many farmers and working people were enraged by the extraordinary wealth that "robber barons" such as Cornelius Vanderbilt and Andrew Carnegie were beginning to show off in sixty-room mansions, two-hundred-foot steam-powered yachts, and six-course dinner banquets. Some of these "Captains of Industry" had used bribery and ruthless business practices in their climb to the top, which infuriated those whose hold on farms and jobs was slipping. By the centennial year, the stage was set for conflicts that would pit the dispossessed against the prosperous and powerful. In these clashes Na-

Taking pride in a century of American achievements, Uncle Sam stands atop one of the Philadelphia Exposition pavilions in this poster from the Centennial Year, 1876.
Courtesy of the Library of Congress, LC-USZ 62-106472.

tive Americans, businessmen, and farmers all used the Founding Fathers as weapons.

☞ A Century of Dishonor

On June 25, 1876, a little over a month after Philadelphia's Centennial Exposition opened, General George Armstrong Custer and 265 U.S. Army cavalrymen were killed by Sioux Indian braves at the Battle of the Little Big Horn in the Dakota Territory. News of the defeat shocked and outraged white Americans, who called for revenge. But "Custer's Last Stand" was one of the few victories Indians won, and one of their very last in 250 years of bloody sporadic warfare between Native Americans and white settlers. By the nation's hundredth birthday, the government had forced many tribes off their ancestral hunting lands and herded them onto bleak reservations to make room for white settlers, land companies, and railroads. Fourteen years later, at the so-called Battle of Wounded Knee, the Army shot down some 150 Sioux men, women, and children, effectively breaking the resistance of the last Plains tribes.

Most Americans believed that Indians were an obstacle to the spread of a "superior" white civilization across the continent. Popular books like Henry D. Northrop's *Indian Horrors or, Massacres by the Red Men,* published in 1891, depicted Native Americans as bloodthirsty savages who had no place in a white man's country. "That the Indians are doomed to extinction," Northrop declared, "that they must disappear as the buffaloes have disappeared before advancing civilization, till all that shall be left of them will be a few little communities scattered here and there . . . cannot be doubted by any one who knows the history of the world."

Northrop and others looked back to the warfare of the American Revolution to justify white attitudes toward Indians. Yes, it was true that a few tribes—the Mashpee of Massachusetts, the Tuscarora and Oneida in New York, and others—had fought with the colonists against the British. But the most formidable tribes, including the Mohawk, Onondaga, Cayuga, and Seneca of the powerful Iroquois Confederation, had sided with the British, hoping that King George III would keep colonial settlers from taking Indian land. Led by their chief Thayendanegea (also known as Joseph Brant), whom the revolutionaries "associated with every thing bloody, ferocious, and hateful," the Mohawk launched surprise attacks against patriot settlements on the New York and Pennsylvania frontiers. Women and children as well as soldiers were killed or taken prisoner by Indians and redcoats in these raids.

By the late nineteenth century, many Americans knew the story of young

The murder of Jane McCrea by Wyandot Indians, painted by the artist John Vanderlyn twenty-seven years after the event. Courtesy of the Wadsworth Atheneum, Hartford, Connecticut.

Jane McCrea, who had been murdered and scalped at Fort Edward, New York, by Wyandot Indian allies of the British general "Gentleman Johnny" Burgoyne. McCrea was actually engaged to be married to a Tory officer on Burgoyne's staff, and the killing had been a mistake. But in the years after the Revolution, as wartime hatred of loyalist "traitors" faded, Americans cared less that McCrea's lover had fought against independence than that she had been brutally killed by Indian "savages." Her gruesome death was immortalized in a poem that told how

> The cursed Indian *knife, the cruel blade,*
> *Had cut her scalp, they'd tore it from her head;*
> *The blood is gushing forth from all her veins,*
> *With bitter groans and sighs she tells her pains.*

The poem reinforced nineteenth-century Americans in their belief that Indians had always threatened vulnerable whites on the frontier, including women and children, just as they continued to attack western settlers in the years after the Civil War.

Yet Northrop and others who dwelled on atrocities had only told part of the story. Many of the leaders of the American Revolution were fascinated by Native Americans, although their feelings were often mixed. In 1754, before the Revolution, when Benjamin Franklin was urging the colonies to act together in order to strengthen themselves, he asked them to follow the example of the Iroquois Confederation, whose tribes had been politically united for almost two centuries. Even so, Franklin had to remind his white audience that Indians were "inferior." "It would be a strange thing," Franklin stated, "if Six Nations of ignorant savages should be capable of forming a scheme for such a union, . . . and yet that a like union should be impracticable for ten or a dozen English colonies, to whom it is more necessary and must be more advantageous."

Thomas Jefferson was extremely impressed by Native American achievements. He believed that Indians were equal to whites "in mind as well as in body," and he felt that the eloquence of the Mingo chief Logan rivaled that of the great orators of ancient Greece.

During the Revolutionary War, however, attacks by white Americans on Indian villages often matched or exceeded the atrocities committed by Indians against whites. Seeking to avenge Iroquois raids, General Washington ordered his troops to "cut off their settlements, destroy their next Years crops, and do them every other mischief which time and circumstances will permit." In response, American soldiers massacred Native American communities in New York and Pennsylvania, sometimes butchering pro-American as well as pro-British tribes. After one such attack, the Onondaga chief Tioguanda described how the Americans "put to death all the Women and Children, excepting some of the Young Women that they carried away for the use of their soldiers, and were put to death in a more shameful and Scandalous manner. . . . Tho' they call themselves Christians, they are more cruel than the Indians who are not so."

Although Franklin admitted that "almost every war between the Indians and whites has been occasioned by some injustice of the latter towards the former," the Founders of the United States did little to protect the Indians from land-hungry whites after the Revolution was over. "The robbery, the cruelty which were done under the cloak of this hundred years of treaty-making and treaty-breaking, are greater than can be told," Helen Hunt Jackson declared in her book *A Century of Dishonor*, published in 1881.

Jackson was a white writer from Massachusetts who had decided to look carefully at the way the government had treated Indian tribes in the hundred years since the Declaration of Independence. What she found was that from the very start, the leaders of the Revolution and the new republic had broken their promises to Indians. As president, George Washington had assured tribes that they would be treated as independent nations, and that "the General Government will never consent to your being defrauded; but it will protect you in all your just rights." In 1795 the president's negotiators told the leaders of twelve tribes that "the heart of General Washington, the Great Chief of America, wishes for nothing so much as peace and brotherly love," and that white officials were "acting the part of a tender father to them and their children in thus providing for them not only at present, but forever."

The reality was far different. Government agents made treaty after treaty with the Indians, guaranteeing their right to their land. But when white settlers desired Indian lands for themselves, the government broke these treaties, allowing the settlers into Indian territories and forcing the tribes to move farther west. Tribes that had fought for American independence were displaced along with those that had fought with the British. It was hard for Indians to see the Founding Fathers as very fatherly when one result of the American Revolution was the loss of their land. As one Delaware chief told President Washington's representatives when they asked the Delaware to give up some of their hunting grounds, "You have talked to us about concessions. It appears strange that you should expect any from us, who have only been defending our just rights against your invasions."

The Cherokee of Georgia and Alabama were considered among the most "civilized" of the tribes. By the early years of the nineteenth century their communities boasted schools and churches, and they had started a newspaper, *The Phoenix*, published in their own language. They had created their own system of tribal government based on the U.S. Constitution, complete with executive, legislative, and judicial branches. President Jefferson promised the Cherokee that "you may always rely on the counsel and assistance of the United States." Yet by the 1820s and 1830s, white settlers and land speculators were eager for their lands. In 1837 and 1838, U.S. government troops forced over fifteen thousand Cherokee to leave their homes and move eight hundred miles west to "Indian Territory" in Oklahoma. One out of every four Cherokee men, women, and children died on this "Trail of Tears."

For the Cherokee, as for other Indians, the American Revolution and the nation it created were a disaster. In 1822 the Cherokee had appealed to the U.S. Senate to honor its treaties with the tribe. Their leaders noted that they were asking for justice "under that memorable declaration, 'that all men are created equal; that they are endowed by their Creator with certain inalienable rights; that among these are life, liberty, and the pursuit of happiness.'" But the governor of Georgia denounced their message as "insults from the polluted lips of outcasts and vagabonds," and the Cherokee lost their land. The lesson, Helen Hunt Jackson argued, was clear: Americans cherished the words and ideals of the Founding Fathers—except when Native Americans dared to speak them.

☞ Hamilton the Hero

While Indians and their defenders remembered one version of the American Revolution, wealthy white gentlemen and ladies recalled another. The Revolution "was no wild breaking away from all authority," Robert C. Winthrop, a Boston politician, asserted in an Independence Day speech in 1876. "It was no mad revolt against every thing like government. . . . There was a respect for the great principles of Law and Order."

In the years after the Civil War, businessmen and politicians like Winthrop presented their own version of the Revolution to the public. Their vision of an expanding industrial America held little room for Indians. They also rejected the interpretations of labor leaders, black activists, and feminists who saw the Revolution as an uprising organized by "radicals" who had wanted to expand the rights of workers, blacks, and women. In Winthrop's hometown in 1887, as in William Nell's day thirty years earlier, historians and politicians tried to stop the erection of a monument dedicated to the five men killed in the Boston Massacre. Those men, after all, had been mere rioters, while the *true* patriots had defended American liberties by orderly and lawful methods before resorting to violence. Besides, one of the five was Crispus Attucks, a black man, and another, Patrick Carr, had been an Irish Catholic immigrant—hardly the kinds of Americans to represent an event as important as the Revolution! The statue was erected, but not without grumbling and opposition.

While it was true that Thomas Paine's *Common Sense* had helped to produce the Declaration of Independence, conservatives argued Paine was too dangerous a man to be considered a hero, especially in an era when his radical ideas might inspire labor unions and immigrant "troublemakers" to challenge the right of the rich to enjoy their wealth. Not only was Paine a godless infidel, one historian wrote, but "of all the human kind he was the filthiest and the nastiest, and his disgusting habits grew upon him with his years."

Instead, the true heroes of the Revolution had been men like themselves, merchants like John Hancock, self-made businessmen like Benjamin Franklin, lawyers like Gouverneur Morris and John Jay, and prosperous landowners like George Washington. Yes, these men had desired independence from Britain. But once independence was achieved, their property and education gave them the right to lead American society, without too much interference from the "common people" below. *These* Founding Fathers had wisely created a society in which merchants, bankers, and manufacturers had free rein to make America into the powerful industrial nation it had become by its hundredth birthday.

One Founding Father, Alexander Hamilton, became especially popular among many businessmen and those Americans who agreed with their vision of America in the years after the Civil War. Brilliant but arrogant, charming yet impatient with those who disagreed with him, Hamilton fascinated Americans in the late nineteenth century. It was hard to be neutral about his dashing but tragically short life. As one of his biographers put it, "he was loved and hated with equal intensity."

Born on the island of Nevis in the Caribbean in either 1755 or 1757, the illegitimate son of a Scottish immigrant and the daughter of a plantation owner, Hamilton moved to New York City at age sixteen to study at King's College (which is now Columbia University). Eager for fame and power, he joined the revolutionary movement, becoming an artillery officer and then General Washington's secretary and aide during the War for Independence. After the war, Hamilton served a term as one of New York's representatives in Congress and settled into a career as a successful Wall Street lawyer. His intelligence, charm, and ability as a speaker impressed all who encountered him in the legislative chamber or the courtroom.

"I am persuaded," Hamilton declared, "that a firm union is as necessary to perpetuate our liberties as it is to make us respectable." He believed that only a strong national government could guarantee the future prosperity and power of the new United States.

More than any other American, Hamilton was responsible for the Constitution of 1787. He was the first to propose that a Convention meet in Philadelphia to consider changing the Articles of Confederation. When the assembled delegates created the Constitution and with it a new and daring scheme of government, Hamilton, James Madison, and John Jay wrote *The Federalist Papers* to urge Americans to ratify this plan for a stronger, more unified United States.

Selected by George Washington in 1789 to be the first secretary of the treasury, Hamilton plunged into the work of forging a financial structure for the new federal government. He established the Bank of the United States, which created a national currency and credit system. He persuaded Congress to levy taxes to provide revenues for the new government.

He also issued a Report on Manufactures that called for Congress to support industrial development. Even though he had fought to make America independent from Britain, Hamilton greatly admired England's industrial strength. "Not only the wealth," he maintained, "but the independence and security of a Country, appear to be materially connected with the prosperity of manufactures." Rather than letting America remain a nation of farmers, Hamilton wanted it to become a society of great manufacturing and mercantile cities. He believed that if Congress encouraged Americans to build factories, the United States would rise to become a great industrial power rivaling England.

Even though he believed in the republican form of government, Hamilton distrusted the common people of America. "The people are turbulent and changing," he was quoted as saying during the Constitutional Convention of 1787, "they seldom judge or determine right." History, Hamilton claimed, proved that governments could be *too* democratic. When that happened, the common people threatened to become "an ungovernable mob." Hamilton feared that if the ordinary farmers and tradesmen had their way, they would keep the national government weak and disorganized. He also believed that when the common people held power, they passed unfair laws that victimized the wealthy minority of the population.

To cure what he called the "disease" of "democracy," Hamilton believed that men like himself and those he associated with—the rich merchants, lawyers, and manufacturers of New York, Philadelphia, Boston, and other coastal cities—should be entrusted with political leadership in America. Only propertied gentlemen were sure to possess the knowledge, stability of character, and concern for order that could guarantee the survival of the new nation. The fact that businessmen invested in the bonds issued by his Treasury Department, Hamilton argued, ensured that the most powerful and wealthy men in America would be interested in keeping the national government healthy and strong.

Many Americans were infuriated by Hamilton's views and plans. His critics charged that Hamilton was trying to "overwhelm and destroy . . . every free and valuable principle of our government." In the early 1790s Thomas Jefferson and the Democratic-Republicans opposed Hamilton's policies. Jefferson and his allies believed that it was up to the common people, the farmers and artisans, to keep the federal government from getting too powerful. In the eyes of Democratic-Republicans, Hamilton seemed to be introducing into America "the corrupt and wretched system of British politics and finance," and creating "an accumulation of great wealth in a few hands."

Hamilton and his followers in the Federalist Party argued that, rather than being the people's enemy, he was a friend of the common folk, whose plans for a stronger government would bring them safety and prosperity. But Hamilton's political career was cut short abruptly in 1804. In that year, Vice President Aaron Burr challenged him to a duel for making "dishonorable" statements about Burr's character. On a July morning at Weehawken, New Jersey, on a bluff overlooking the Hudson River, Burr shot and killed the man who had created the nation's financial system and prepared the United States for its future as an industrial and commercial giant. Hamilton was not yet fifty years old.

The brilliant and dashing Alexander Hamilton, portrayed in 1804, the year of his fatal duel with Aaron Burr. Courtesy of the National Portrait Gallery, Smithsonian Institution.

As America took its place as one of the world's leading industrial powers in the years after the Civil War, biographers and historians celebrated Hamilton for his foresight. "He was a leader," the politician and writer Henry Cabot Lodge declared. "He could mark out a path and walk in it, and if the people hesitated or held back, he would walk alone." The country's greatness, Lodge and others claimed, was fostered by big businessmen who dared to imagine the country as a leading producer and exporter of manufactured goods, and by a strong national government that would guarantee that American interests would be respected internationally. Lodge himself later became a powerful U.S. senator, and with his friend Theodore Roosevelt would work to extend America's economic and military influence around the globe. Hamilton was their hero: "He alone perceived the destiny which was in store for the republic . . . in his task of founding a government he also founded a nation. It was a great work."

☞ *Wall Street Owns the Country*

"Wall Street owns the country," Mary E. Lease declared to an audience of Kansas farmers in 1890. "It is no longer a government of the people, by the people, and for the people, but a government of Wall Street, by Wall Street, and for Wall Street . . . The great common people of this country are slaves . . . The West and South are bound and prostrate before the manufacturing East."

Lease was an organizer for a political movement that swept the farms of the West and the South at the end of the nineteenth century. Across the wheat fields of the Plains states, and in the cotton fields of the South, on land that had once belonged to Indian tribes, farmers were struggling to keep their farms from failing and their families out of poverty. They blamed wealthy businessmen for their troubles, and rejected Alexander Hamilton's vision of an America run by merchants and industrialists. In 1892 they formed the Populist Party to fight for their own, very different vision of what America should be.

Populists blamed railroad owners, bankers, and merchants for their

The spirits of Washington, Jefferson, and Lincoln look on in horror as big business lords over America. This Populist cartoon was published in an Oklahoma newspaper, the Norman People's Voice, *in 1894.* Courtesy of the University of Oklahoma Press.

problems. At corporate headquarters in distant cities like Chicago, Pittsburgh, and New York, wealthy railroad magnates secretly collaborated to limit competition and keep freight rates high, forcing helpless western farmers to pay more and more to ship their crops to market. Railroad officials bribed corrupt representatives in state legislatures to make sure that government regulation would not interfere with their profits. Farmers who had to borrow money from banks to finance their planting ran the risk of losing their family farms if they could not repay the loans. In the South, many farmers, both black and white, went into debt to local store owners who sold them overpriced goods and tools supplied by Northern merchants. These farmers often had to give over their crops and even their land to pay their debts, sinking each year further into poverty and dependence on the shopkeeper. Though freed from slavery since the Civil War, Southern black farmers found themselves especially at risk: Those who dared to challenge exploitation by white businessmen faced violence at the hands of the racist Ku Klux Klan or lynch mobs.

"Those who labour in the earth," Thomas Jefferson had written, "are the chosen people of God, if ever he had a chosen people . . . Let our work-shops remain in Europe." Relying on their own land and hard work, Jefferson claimed, farmers made the best and most independent citizens. A country life was more healthy and less open to corruption than the urban life led by merchants, industrialists, and factory workers. "When we get piled upon one another in large cities, as in Europe, we shall become corrupt, as in Europe," he had written to James Madison. Jefferson wanted the United States to remain a nation of farmers, with few large cities, few factories, and few powerful businessmen.

But something had gone terribly wrong, farmers maintained as they flocked into the Populist Party. Alexander Hamilton's bankers and manufacturers were taking over the country, squeezing farmers for their land and money. Populists rallied to save their America, the America that the "Sage of Monticello" had celebrated one hundred years before.

James "Cyclone" Davis of Texas was one of the Populists' most effective orators. He held rural audiences spellbound as he quoted from the published

"I feed you all." *Jefferson's idea of an America where farmers were the most important citizens is echoed in this 1876 print.* Courtesy of the Library of Congress, LC-USZ 62-2364.

Works of Jefferson, piled in a stack next to him on the podium. Dressed in a black coat and vest, trousers, and alligator boots, with a black sombrero in his hand, Davis told farmers that their struggle for America was the same one that Jefferson and his allies had waged against Hamilton's Federalists a century earlier. Jefferson had trusted the common people to elect representatives and run the government. Hamilton, on the other hand, had believed that "the people were unsafe . . . that they should have as little to do with government as possible . . . that the wealthy classes should rule the masses; that an aristocracy should hold the offices and rule the people."

Davis and other Populist leaders vowed to win America back from the "aristocrats of business." To do so, they proposed wide-ranging and radical reforms. The Populist Party argued that the federal government should take over ownership and control of the railroads from private corporations in order to guarantee fair and reasonable freight rates. Populists also advocated measures to make state legislatures more responsive to the wishes of ordinary voters and to eliminate corruption by wealthy business interests. To get these measures passed, the Populists organized farmers to vote and win elections. In 1892 their presidential candidate, James Weaver, won over one million votes (losing to Democrat Grover Cleveland), while voters elected Populist governors, congressmen, and state legislators in several Western and Southern states.

In reality, the Populists weren't always as Jeffersonian or democratic as they claimed to be. Jefferson, who feared giving too much power of any kind to the federal government, probably would have been horrified by the idea of the United States owning and running the railroads. And white Populist leaders upheld racial inequalities, forcing African-American farmers to join a segregated Colored Farmers' Alliance rather than welcoming them into mainstream Populist organizations. But Populists maintained that they were true to Jefferson's larger vision of America as an "Empire of Liberty" governed by and for farmers. In 1896 Populists again had their eyes on the presidency.

The choice they made that year has remained controversial ever since. Rather than running their own man, Populists endorsed the Democratic Party candidate, William Jennings Bryan of Nebraska, in the hope that the two parties united could defeat the pro-business Republican nominee, William McKinley. It was easy for Populist farmers to like Bryan. He declared that "I would have history say of me: He did what he could to make the Government what Jefferson desired it to be." Speaking at the Democratic national convention in Chicago, Bryan reminded Americans that farmers, not greedy businessmen, actually fed the nation: "Destroy our farms, and the grass will grow in the streets of every city in the country."

The Democratic Party platform called for the federal government to add silver to the gold coinage in the national money supply. This would increase

When William Jennings Bryan ran again for the presidency in 1908, this campaign souvenir allowed voters to see him as a "second Washington." Courtesy of the National Portrait Gallery, Smithsonian Institution.

the amount of money in circulation, which would make it easier for farmers to pay back bank loans at lower interest rates. Many Populists liked this idea. But Bryan ignored most of the other reforms proposed by the Populists in order to focus on his "free silver" campaign. Meanwhile, businessmen in the large cities mobilized to defeat him. They viewed the typical Populist as a "shabby, wild-eyed, rattlebrained fanatic," and were appalled by the idea that a man endorsed by the Populists might be elected president. Wealthy industrialists and financiers poured millions of dollars into McKinley's campaign and into the Republican Party.

On election day, McKinley won a landslide victory over Bryan. Populists were devastated by the defeat. Although Bryan ran for the presidency on the

Democratic ticket two more times, the Populist Party never regained its momentum. Farmers continued to fight for regulation of the railroads and clean government, but never again were they able to organize a national political movement as powerful and militant as the Populists. As much as they kept their faith in the America envisioned by Thomas Jefferson, many had to admit that the America of Alexander Hamilton—industrial, commercial, and urban—was the America of the future.

In different ways, Native Americans and farmers both felt that their America was being taken away from them. Reminding other Americans that Jefferson had written the Declaration of Independence for the sake of "freedom" and "equality" did not restore what they were losing. But many who felt betrayed and abandoned by what the country had become continued to argue and fight for their visions of what it should be. In a new century, the struggle over the meaning of the Founding Fathers—and of the United States—would continue to be fought.

One Hundred Percent Americans

IMMIGRANTS AND ANCESTORS

☞ *A Golden Door?*

On the afternoon of October 28, 1886, one million people lined the decks of boats and the piers of New York Harbor to witness the dedication of the Statue of Liberty Enlightening the World. In a cold and misty rain, President Grover Cleveland disembarked from the battleship U.S.S. *Despatch* onto Bedloe's Island, the site of the new statue, as a 21-gun salute roared from the eight warships of the navy's Atlantic Squadron anchored nearby. Arrayed in the waters of the bay surrounding the island was a flotilla of some three hundred sailboats, steamers, yachts, and tugboats crowded with thousands of people eager to see the statue's unveiling. At three o'clock, as hundreds of steam-whistle blasts filled the air and as a military band struck up "My Country, 'tis of Thee," Frédéric-Auguste Bartholdi, the statue's creator, pulled a rope attached to a rain-drenched red, white, and blue flag covering the statue's head and revealed the face of Liberty to the world.

The Statue of Liberty was a gift from the government of France to the United States, a symbol of the friendship that united the two republics. The bond between the two nations was of long standing. France supplied troops, ships, and money that had enabled the new United States to win its independence from Britain during the Revolutionary War. In turn, the principles of the American Declaration of Independence had helped to ignite France's own revolution of 1789. To commemorate this bond, the statue held in her left arm a tablet bearing the date July 4, 1776, in roman numerals.

In his speech accepting the gift, President Cleveland envisioned the statue "keeping watch and ward before the open gates of America." Cleveland's phrase was appropriate, for New York Harbor had indeed proved a gateway into the United States for millions of immigrants, and millions more would arrive in the decades after the statue's dedication. The poet Emma Lazarus portrayed the statue welcoming into America future generations of refugees from poverty and persecution:

> *Give me your tired, your poor,*
> *Your huddled masses yearning to breathe free,*
> *The wretched refuse of your teeming shore.*
> *Send these, the homeless, tempest-tost to me,*
> *I lift my lamp beside the golden door.*

But in the late nineteenth and early twentieth centuries, not all Americans were sure that the golden door should be kept open. Between 1881 and 1900, nearly nine million people immigrated to the U.S. In the first decade of the twentieth century, another 8.7 million arrived. By 1910 one out of every three Americans had been born abroad or had at least one foreign-born parent. Many native-born citizens wondered whether such unrestricted immigration was a good thing. Earlier generations of immigrants from Ireland and Germany had already brought alien customs and traditions into the country. Now they were joined by millions of poor peasant families from Italy, the Russian Empire, Austria-Hungary, and the Balkans, whose religious beliefs, political attitudes, languages, dress, and diet seemed even more strange and outlandish.

To make matters worse, millions of these newcomers settled in large cities like New York and Chicago, where their labor fueled American factories but where immigrant neighborhoods soon filled with disease-ridden and overcrowded slums. By relying on the votes of the foreign born, corrupt political "bosses" were able to take over city governments. Many worried that the urban centers would become "foreign cities," with no place in them for native-born Americans.

"Can we absorb such a heterogeneous mass of humanity, give them power to vote, and still keep the purity of our institutions?" This was the question posed by a speaker at the national conference of the Daughters of the American Revolution in 1892. A writer for the *American Tribune* newspaper put it more bluntly: "What good results," he asked, could be achieved "by the presence of our foreign born rotten banana sellers, thieving rag dealers, Italian organ grinders, Chinese washmen and Bohemian coal miners," whose very breath "would make a dog vomit?"

The immigrants themselves saw things differently. Many viewed America as a land of opportunity and freedom, a country that would deliver on the promises of "life, liberty, and the pursuit of happiness" that the Declaration of Independence guarantees and that the Statue represents. Foreign-born men, women, and children labored long hours at subsistence wages in factories and "sweatshops" in order to survive and, they hoped, save up a little money for the future. Most struggled to "become American," to learn the new country's language and customs, while continuing to hold on to "Old World" traditions that still had meaning for them.

Both immigrants and established Americans turned to the American Revolution to help define the America they hoped would emerge in the early twentieth century. Not surprisingly, they came up with different and sometimes conflicting understandings of what the Revolution meant. As America became more and more a society of different languages, religions, and customs brought from abroad, natives and immigrants argued over the event that had created the nation and unified Americans in the first place.

☞ *Our Own Heroes*

Wasn't it time, a speaker asked the delegates to the national convention of the Sons of the American Revolution (S.A.R.) in 1890, for native-born men to work for "a recognition of the rights of Americans, as better than the rights of ignorant foreigners?" The S.A.R. was one of several patriotic organizations established by native-born men and women in the late nineteenth century, as immigration increased. To join the S.A.R. or the D.A.R. (Daughters of the

American Revolution) an applicant had to prove that he or she had an ancestor who had fought in the American Revolution.

By linking themselves to their revolutionary forefathers, such "blue bloods" set themselves apart from what one of them described as "the millions of poor and ignorant pouring into our commonwealth." While the new immigrants were poor Catholics, Eastern Orthodox Christians, and Jews from southern and eastern Europe, members of the S.A.R. and D.A.R. were mostly middle-class and wealthy Protestants whose own ancestors had come from the British Isles generations before.

S.A.R. and D.A.R. members felt nostalgic for an America they believed Jefferson, Washington, and their own ancestors had fought for in the Revolution. This was an America of small towns and honest politics, where people knew their neighbors and came together in town meetings to make the laws. Immigrants, they felt, threatened this America. Some native-born Protestants blamed immigrants for the rise of crime-ridden big cities and political corruption. They seldom paused to consider that the foreign-born were the victims as well as a cause of such changes.

In their speeches and celebrations of national holidays, some S.A.R. and D.A.R. members implied that the United States, which their ancestors had fought to create, really belonged to them. It was *their* responsibility to make sure that America would not be contaminated by foreigners. Some of the patriotic societies called for federal laws to limit or halt immigration from Europe. At the same time, they worked to educate those immigrants who had already arrived.

"The millions of aliens in the United States are being taught what the nation stands for," the S.A.R. announced in 1911. "The immigrants of today may be the good Americans of tomorrow, if they are made to know their privileges and their duties in their adopted country." The S.A.R. handed out one million leaflets on the duties of American citizenship in Italian, Polish, Hungarian, Yiddish, Greek, and nine other languages in immigrant neighborhoods. The societies placed portraits of George Washington in city classrooms filled with the children of immigrants, and encouraged the foreign born to read the Dec-

Members of the Sons of the Revolution gather at New York's Fraunces Tavern in 1883, a century after General George Washington bid farewell to his troops there at the close of the Revolution. Courtesy of the Fraunces Tavern Museum, New York, New York.

laration of Independence and Benjamin Franklin's *Autobiography* as they learned English.

By encouraging immigrants to learn about the American Revolution and to revere its leaders, the S.A.R. also hoped to teach them to respect and obey the native-born Protestant men who remained at the top of American society: the businessmen, industrialists, educators, and politicians who were themselves the descendants of the early colonists and revolutionaries. Such men might value immigrants as workers in their factories or as voters, but they did not relish the idea of foreign-born "agitators" challenging their control of industry and politics. S.A.R. members believed that if the values of *their* Revolution were taught to immigrants, then the newcomers would turn away from radical political ideas, labor unions, and other "dangerous" influences.

Martha Washington helps to sell shoes to Czech immigrants in their own language: an ad published in Chicago, 1916. From THE KATOLIK CESKO-AMERICKY KALENDER.

Courtesy of the Immigration History Research Center, University of Minnesota.

Immigrants were often eager to learn the lessons of American history and government taught in adult-education classes sponsored by the patriotic societies, as well as by their own immigrant-aid organizations. To understand the accomplishments of George Washington and Thomas Jefferson was to take a step closer to becoming a true "Yankee," a real American who didn't have to feel ashamed of his or her foreign accent.

But as immigrants, and the children and grand-children of immigrants, became more secure in their new homeland and more familiar with American history, they began to realize that the Revolution had been theirs as well. Soon immigrants started demanding that patriotic heroes of foreign birth be discussed in school textbooks, and that statues be erected in their honor. As one Irish-American put it, "We were foreign. We did not feel at home. But we began to know. We began to feel at home. We learned of our race's participation in the up-building of the nation. We will prove our part in America's history; then the children as Americans can feel as Americans."

"The first woman to fight for American liberty . . . was Margaret Cochran, an Irishwoman," Michael J. O'Brien of the American Irish Historical Society

A 1907 cartoon uses ethnic stereotypes to show how various immigrant and racial groups supposedly recast Washington as one of their own. It also lampoons President Roosevelt's aggressive Philippine policy. Courtesy of the Ellis Island Immigration Museum.

proudly asserted in 1917. Cochran took her husband's place after he was killed at the Battle of Fort Washington in 1776. "She was not that type of woman who picked up her apron and filled it with tears," O'Brien noted. "She knew how to handle a gun." Irish settlers, both Protestant and Catholic, had been a significant minority in the colonies, and many had done their share during the Revolution. "Irishmen and their sons," O'Brien told an applauding audience of Irish-Americans in Chicago, ". . . answered the clarion call of patriotism and came to fight, as Irishmen know how to fight, to help make this country a free and independent nation."

Irish-Americans who were Catholic felt a special need to remind their fellow citizens of their part in creating the United States. A long tradition of Protestant bigotry had kept many Irish Catholic immigrants out of decent jobs in the nineteenth century, and had even triggered bloody religious riots in American cities. Like African-Americans, who had earlier revived the memory of Crispus Attucks, Irish-Americans now honored such revolutionary heroes as General John Sullivan, the son of Irish indentured servants, in order to challenge "prejudiced historians" who had downplayed the Irish contribution to the nation's history. Americans of Irish Catholic descent also used the Revolution to show loyalty to their relatives in the homeland who were struggling to free Ireland from British rule in the 1900s and 1910s. Irish colonists had helped their fellow Americans win independence from Britain in 1776, Michael O'Brien maintained; now, in 1917, it was up to the United States to help Ireland do the same.

Very few Poles had settled in the colonies before the American Revolution. But the growing numbers of Polish immigrants at the turn of the century could still celebrate their own revolutionary heroes. Two Polish volunteers, Tadeusz Kosciuszko and Casimir Pulaski, had commanded troops in Washington's army. Kosciuszko became one of the most important military engineers on the American side, while the dashing horseman Pulaski had led American cavalry into battle and was killed by British cannon fire at the seige of Savannah, Georgia, in 1779.

As they marched off to battle in Cuba during the Spanish-American War of 1898, such volunteer units as the Kosciuszko Guard of Milwaukee, composed of Polish immigrants, proudly honored the memory of the revolutionary officers. "Our own hero Kosciuszko," a Polish Catholic priest told them, "came to America in order that colonists might shake the yoke of oppression

Proud to be European, proud to be American. Heroes from Polish history and Catholic saints flank Washington, Pulaski, and Kosciuszko in this Polish-American poster printed in 1891. Courtesy of the Library of Congress, LC-USZ 62-60639.

"Betsy Ross" teaches the "huddled masses." Immigrant women learn about loyalty during a citizenship class in a New York City classroom. (In reality, the story of Betsy Ross's making a flag for George Washington was rooted more in folklore than fact.) Courtesy of Brown Brothers, Sterling, Pennsylvania.

from their shoulders—win freedom from the English crown. And now, you men are going on a familiar mission, to help win freedom from the tyranny of the Spaniards." Polish-Americans also remembered the two heroes when they supported the movement to create an independent Poland, free from the rule of Russia, Germany, and Austria-Hungary, the three empires that controlled Polish territory in the early twentieth century. During World War I, thousands of young Polish-Americans joined "an army of Kosciuszko" in Europe, hoping to liberate their homeland in the name of the revolutionary freedom fighter.

American Jews also honored their forefathers who had fought for the revolutionary cause. While there had been only small numbers of Jews living in the colonies, Jewish patriots such as Benjamin Nones and Isaac Franks of Philadelphia had risked their lives fighting for American independence. Starting in 1903, Jewish veterans placed American flags each Memorial Day on the graves of eighteen soldiers of the Revolution buried in the old Hebrew cemetery in New York City.

But the most popular revolutionary hero among Jewish-Americans was not a soldier. Haym Salomon, an immigrant businessman from Poland, lent money without charging interest to members of the Continental Congress at a time when funds were scarce and the economy of the revolutionary United States was in a shambles. Salomon also spied on the British and helped American prisoners of war to escape from redcoat-occupied New York. In the early twentieth century, when most new Jewish immigrants were from Poland and Eastern Europe, newcomers could point with pride at the patriotism and generosity of one of their own. A group of American Jews made this clear in 1930 when they formed a committee to erect a statue of Salomon in New York City: "The figure of the Polish immigrant Jew will rise in granite to testify as a symbol of Jewry's participation and aid when America was born."

Having fled religious persecution in Europe, American Jews reminded their fellow citizens that the revolutionaries had fought to create a nation dedicated to the idea of religious freedom. During the national centennial in July 1876, a group of prominent American rabbis traveled to Mount Vernon in order to plant a tree by George Washington's grave. The rabbis read from a copy of the letter President Washington had written to a synagogue congregation in Newport, Rhode Island, in 1790. Noting that the United States government "gives to bigotry no sanction, to persecution no assistance," Washington had concluded with a wish: "May the Children of the stock of Abraham, who dwell in this land, continue to merit and enjoy the good will of the other inhabitants; while every one shall sit in safety under his own vine and fig tree, and there shall be none to make him afraid."

For "ethnics" as for "blue bloods," revolutionary ancestors were not obscure, dimly remembered figures. They were living symbols, sources of pride and identity. Yet ancestors meant different things to different Americans. Some native Protestants continued to view the Revolution as private property. The patriotism of their great-great-grandparents, they insisted, was proof of their own superiority and their right to run the country. When, on the other hand,

Irish-, Polish-, and Jewish-Americans found forebears among the patriots of 1776, they demanded a place in the history books—and in a changing American society.

☞ *Wartime Propaganda*

In the early twentieth century, no group was more proud of their role in the Revolution than German-Americans. By the 1910s, there were over two million German immigrants in the United States—more than any other foreign-born group—and millions of other Americans were descendants of German immigrants. At the time of the Revolution, Germans already made up almost ten percent of the colonial population. Many had been indentured servants who agreed to work seven years without pay for colonial masters in exchange for ship fare from Europe. Once freed from their bondage, these settlers valued the freedom and economic opportunity that the New World provided, and many fought with conviction for American independence. "Families of German descent frequently gave every able-bodied man into the service of the cause," the German-American historian Albert Faust asserted in 1909.

The most famous German hero of the Revolution was Baron Friedrich Wilhelm von Steuben, a colorful, eccentric immigrant who joined General Washington's staff at Valley Forge in the winter of 1778. A veteran of the staff of King Frederick the Great of Prussia, Steuben volunteered to teach Washington's ragtag regiments of untrained farmers how to march and train in the manner of Europe's professional armies. Unable to speak English, Steuben personally drilled a model team of one hundred soldiers, bellowing and cursing in German (translated by interpreters) at their lack of discipline. The Americans laughed at his curses but came to respect his instruction, which they passed on to the other troops. The drill manual that he prepared became the most consulted book in the Continental Army, and Washington relied on Steuben as a trusted military adviser. After the revolution, Steuben remained in the United States, where he was given sixteen thousand acres of farmland by New York State in gratitude for his wartime service.

In 1910 German-Americans persuaded Congress to spend fifty thousand dollars to erect a statue of Steuben across from the White House in Lafayette Park, where monuments to General Washington's other foreign-born officers—the Frenchmen Lafayette and Rochambeau and the Pole Kosciuszko—already stood. At the dedication ceremony, President Taft declared that "the Germans who have become American citizens and their descendants may well take pride in this occasion," honoring "the valued contribution made by a German soldier to the cause of American freedom at the time of its birth."

But German-Americans soon found that their loyalty to the principles of the American Revolution did not protect them from anti-immigrant prejudice and violence. In July 1914 World War I began in Europe. German armies poured into Belgium and France, where they were soon locked into four years of bloody trench warfare against the Allied troops of France and England. German U-boats prowled the North Atlantic, torpedoing enemy vessels and the ships of any neutral nation that dared to supply the Allied powers. President Woodrow Wilson, dedicated to keeping the United States from being entangled in a costly foreign war, proclaimed a policy of strict American neutrality. Meanwhile, agents for the English and German governments distributed books, pamphlets, and other propaganda throughout the country in an effort to get the American public and the American government to take sides.

Pro-German writers tried to persuade Americans that the struggle in Europe was a war against English tyranny and arrogance, much like the American Revolution had been. In his magazine *The Fatherland*, George Sylvester Viereck, a German-American poet, asserted that "General George Washington fought the same enemy against whom Germany and the German people are to-day defending their national existence. . . . Would George Washington, would Abraham Lincoln be found on the side of England against Germany, if they were alive to-day?"

Pro-Allied writers responded by reminding Americans that not all Germans had fought on their side during the Revolution. In a book entitled *German Conspiracies in America*, one William H. Skaggs tried to stir up anti-German hatred and pro-Allied enthusiasm by using examples from American

history. He reminded his readers that some thirty thousand German soldiers, known as Hessians, had been hired by George III to fight on the British side during the Revolution. Skaggs tried to make American readers feel that, just as their own forefathers had suffered at the hands of Hessian soldiers in 1776, the people of Europe were being terrorized by German armies in 1914. "The shocking stories of German atrocities during the American Revolution," Skaggs argued, were practically identical to "the details of German atrocities in Belgium during the present war in Europe."

German-Americans had often pointed out that the Hessian troops were virtual slaves of their rulers and had no choice but to follow orders. Many Hessians deserted rather than fight for the redcoats, and large numbers of them stayed in America after the war and became loyal citizens. But Skaggs ignored all this. Instead, the Germans were a "nation of ruthless destroyers." Benjamin Franklin, Skaggs noted, worried that German immigrants might outnumber English settlers in Pennsylvania, making it difficult for Yankees to "preserve our language, and even our government will become precarious."

Skaggs distorted history to serve his anti-German propaganda, just as Viereck had manipulated it to support his anti-English sentiments. Because George III's mother was a German princess and since he was also of German ancestry on his father's side, Skaggs maintained that he was "a typical German . . . brutal and notoriously corrupt." The civilian population of England, he argued, had actually sympathized with the colonists' fight for freedom. In Skaggs's hands, the American Revolution was twisted into a war between English-speaking Americans on one side and George III and his Hessians on the other. The Revolution had really been a struggle between freedom-loving colonists and tyrannical Germans, with the English people supporting the colonists from the sidelines!

While immigrants and their opponents had earlier argued over who the true heroes of the Revolution really were, writers like Viereck and Skaggs now

He fought England, not Germany! The cover of George S. Viereck's pro-German Fatherland, *published in the first months of World War I.* Courtesy of Columbia University Libraries.

deliberately distorted and falsified the facts of the Revolution to win over the American public. The Revolution had become convenient fodder for the makers and manipulators of wartime propaganda.

The Skaggses rather than the Vierecks finally won out. On April 2, 1917, President Wilson asked Congress to declare war on Germany. A shared language, a common commitment to representative government, and strong business ties had already led most Americans to favor England and the Allied cause; German U-boat attacks on American shipping were the final straw. In calling for the mobilization of American troops to be sent to join English and French armies in Europe, Wilson argued that American participation would help to ensure that the Allied war effort would "make the world safe for democracy." Thousands of American men eagerly enlisted and were soon on their way to the front in France.

Many German-Americans were torn between their loyalty to the United States and their strong feelings for their native land. But most ended up supporting the Allied war effort. Whole regiments of German-American soldiers fought bravely against the German Army in France, and two of the war's most popular American heroes—General John "Black Jack" Pershing, commander of all U.S. forces at the front, and Eddie Rickenbacker, an ace fighter pilot—were of German ancestry.

Despite their loyalty to the cause, immigrants and their American-born children faced a wave of wartime suspicion and paranoia. With millions of German-born people living in the United States, and millions more from Germany's wartime ally Austria-Hungary, many Americans panicked. Wouldn't these foreigners betray the United States and help their native countries through sabotage, espionage, and resistance to the war effort? Even President Wilson seemed to endorse a harsh policy toward unreliable immigrants. As America moved toward war, he denounced those among the foreign born "who have poured the poison of disloyalty into the very arteries of our national life. . . . Such creatures of passion, disloyalty, and anarchy must be crushed out."

In response to such fears, "one hundred percent Americanism" was the order of the day. Government agents (and many vigilantes) launched a campaign to enforce total loyalty to the war effort and to suppress even the hint of antiwar or anti-Allied dissent. A huge electric sign hanging over New York's Fifth Avenue demanded "Absolute and Unqualified Loyalty to Our Country." The government went to ridiculous lengths to ensure American allegiance to the Allied cause. A federal judge, for example, stopped production of a silent film entitled "The Spirit of '76." A movie about the revolutionary patriots who had fought British redcoats, the judge reasoned, was now inappropriate, since it might "make us a little bit slack in our loyalty to Great Britain in this great emergency."

No matter what they tried to do to prove their "hundred percent Americanism," German-Americans bore the brunt of wartime fear and anger. Public high-school systems across the country banned the teaching of the German language. "When the Kaiser rings the bell, all the Germans go to hell," teenagers taunted their German-American neighbors. Merchants and advertisers substituted "American" words for "German" ones: sauerkraut became "liberty cabbage," hamburgers became "liberty sandwiches," and German shepherds became "Alsatians." At its worst, the loyalty hysteria turned violent. In April 1918 a young German-American named Robert Prager, who had tried to enlist in the U.S. Navy but had been rejected for medical reasons, was attacked by a mob near St. Louis, Missouri. The mob tied Prager's hands with an American flag, dragged him through the streets, and lynched him in front of a crowd of five hundred cheering people. "I guess nobody can say we aren't loyal now," a jury member shouted after helping to acquit the mob leaders.

The war ended with Allied victory and German defeat seven months later. German-Americans had learned a frightening lesson: All their loyalty, all their pride in the part they had played in building the United States, could not protect them when wartime hysteria stirred up fear and hatred of "foreigners." In response, German-Americans formed the Steuben Society in 1919. Once again, they turned to their revolutionary hero to symbolize the two sides of their identity: devotion to America, and an unwillingness to be ashamed of their love for their mother country. Through its educational programs and celebration of the baron's birthday, September 17, as Steuben Day, the Society made clear what generations of immigrants had already tried to express: They could be good Americans while also holding on to the customs and traditions of their native lands. No matter how fiercely bigots tried to claim American history for themselves, German-Americans and other ethnic groups clung to the Revolution as something that could not be taken away from them.

☞ *Closing the Door*

"One hundred percent Americanism" did not die with the Armistice that ended the war. As the 1920s opened, those Americans whose fear of foreigners and "traitors" was stirred up during the war found other targets than German-Americans for their hatred. Now that Russia was under Communist control, many Americans suspected that Soviet-backed agitators and labor leaders were trying to take over the United States as well. Aided by vigilante groups, government officials arrested or deported Communists and other radicals, many of whom were foreign born. Throughout the country, a revived Ku Klux Klan preached hatred of Catholics, Jews, foreigners, African-Americans, and anyone else who was not white, Anglo-Saxon, and Protestant. The Klan elected politicians in several states, and campaigned for federal laws that would keep "foreign scum" from immigrating to America. On Washington's Birthday in 1924, a Klan leader in Virginia told his audience that if the first president were alive he would join the Klan. Such "one hundred percent Americans" conveniently overlooked the fact that Washington had denounced bigotry when he publicly welcomed Jews in America, and that he had been an honorary member of the Sons of St. Patrick, an organization of Irish immigrants.

"The open gates of America" that President Cleveland had praised in dedicating the Statue of Liberty slammed shut during the 1920s. Responding to public pressure, Congress finally passed a series of laws that drastically cut European immigration to the United States (Chinese and Japanese emigration had already been curtailed). Reflecting prejudice against Catholics and Jews, the laws set restrictive quotas on immigrants from southern and eastern Europe, while favoring newcomers from Protestant western and northern Europe. Hundreds of thousands of people who might have escaped the Holocaust during World War II were doomed to remain in Europe because the United States would not let them in. Only in 1965 did the gates open again with a new federal immigration law. Since that time, millions of people, many from developing non-European countries, have sought opportunity, freedom, and safety in the United States. The ongoing arrival of both legal and illegal immigrants continues to prompt disagreement and controversy over America's role in taking in the "huddled masses" of the world.

While America's "golden door" remained closed for forty years and those who disliked immigrants got their way, Irish-, Polish-, Jewish-, and German-Americans continued to honor their own Founding Fathers and Mothers. By showing pride in their revolutionary heroes, they expressed pride in themselves. This self-respect in the face of prejudice and discrimination encouraged them to keep struggling for acceptance and equal opportunity in America. That struggle made it crucial for the children and grandchildren of immigrants to keep alive the memories of Margaret Cochran, Tadeusz Kosciuszko, Haym Salomon, and Friedrich von Steuben.

A Slobbery Mass of Flubdub

DEBUNKING THE FOUNDERS

☞ *Squirrels in Cages*

"I can't stand Benjamin."   —*D. H. Lawrence, 1923*

"Old Daddy Franklin" represented everything that the English novelist D. H. Lawrence hated. The Founding Father was smug, self-satisfied, a man obsessed with controlling himself, being practical, and making money. Even worse, Franklin never performed one passionate, one reckless, one truly *free* act in his entire life. "The soul of man is a dark vast forest," Lawrence argued, "with wild life in it." But Franklin had deliberately turned his back on the "forest," content to cultivate nothing more than "a neat back garden."

This wouldn't have upset Lawrence so much if Franklin had kept to himself. But instead, "cunning little Ben" and his ideas now dominated American life. Franklin's catchy sayings about industry, thrift, punctuality, and sobriety had turned modern America into a nation of human robots bent on working hard, getting rich, and ignoring every "wild" individual impulse and emotion they might feel. Americans had lost their souls as they controlled themselves to pursue the almighty dollar. "Now look at America," Lawrence complained, "got down by her own barbed wire of shalt-nots, and shut up fast in her own 'productive' machines like millions of squirrels running in millions of cages. It is just a farce."

To the English writer, Franklin had not freed America by signing the Declaration of Independence. Instead, his ideas had enslaved the country, and kept Americans from living as *truly* free individuals. Lawrence was not the only one angry at the Founding Fathers. In the 1920s American writers and intellectuals began to look at the revolutionary leaders with skeptical eyes. Suddenly, heroes like Franklin and Washington seemed flawed, imperfect human beings capable of making mistakes and even of deliberately doing things that were wrong.

Earlier, of course, abolitionists, feminists, and Populists had denounced specific aspects of some of the Founders' actions and beliefs—Washington's and Jefferson's slaveholding, Franklin's neglect of his wife, Hamilton's distrust of the common people. But the new denunciations were more sweeping. The critics of the 1920s looked at the aspects of modern American society that troubled them—greed, selfishness, lack of imagination, the pressure to conform to the demands of a "business civilization"—and found the culprits who were guilty of starting the country along this path: the men of 1776.

☞ A Constitution for the Rich

Charles A. Beard, a historian, had started the critical trend in 1913 when he published a book titled *An Economic Interpretation of the Constitution.* Beard focused on the framing of the Constitution by Hamilton, Franklin, Washington, James Madison, and the fifty-one other delegates at the Constitutional Convention in Philadelphia in 1787. The Constitution, after all, had become the most important document in the daily life of the country. It had laid the ground rules for the federal system of government. As interpreted by the Supreme Court, it acted as a blueprint for determining which laws were acceptable and which unacceptable in a society supposedly dedicated to preserving the liberties of the individual.

But Beard told a different, disturbing story. According to his research, the framers of the Constitution in 1787 had written the document not to preserve the people's freedom, but to protect their own financial interests. The era following the end of the Revolution in 1783 was one of economic instability and social unrest, resulting in Shays' Rebellion, an uprising by Massachusetts farmers who refused to pay debts they owed to wealthy merchants. Fearing that the common farmers and working people might try to strip the rich of their money and privileges, Beard claimed, the Founding Fathers called for a new, stronger "frame of government" in 1787 to replace the weak Articles of Confederation.

The fifty-five delegates to the Philadelphia convention, meeting in secret session so that their proceedings would not become public, had included lawyers, landlords, moneylenders, merchants, manufacturers, and slaveowners, but not a single common farmer or artisan. By creating a strong national government that could raise an army, these Founders ensured that uprisings threatening the lives and property of the wealthy could be crushed. And Beard made a startling discovery when he dug into the dusty records of the Treasury Department in Washington: Forty of the fifty-five men had lent money to the government itself during the Revolution, or bought government bonds after the war when they were cheap. By giving the new federal government the power to collect taxes, they guaranteed that the money they had lent or invested would be repaid to them, and with high interest.

Beard was deeply influenced by socialists and Populists who, in his own time, were questioning the ways in which big businessmen used the Constitution to protect their wealth from challenges by farmers, workers, and reformers. The influence showed in his book. All in all, Beard argued, the Founders had selfishly created a Constitution that really preserved the power of wealthy "gentlemen" while limiting the power of ordinary farmers and working people. Throughout American history, he claimed, wealthy merchants, bankers, and industrialists had tried to keep the common people from gaining a voice in government. American life was really a relentless "war between business and populism."

The Founding Fathers, Beard suggested, had fooled the American people into thinking that they had created a document that protected and guaranteed their liberties. In reality, the Constitution was an undemocratic document that preserved inequality.

Beard's book caused a sensation when it was published. Some saw it as a vicious attack on the memory of the nation's greatest men. SCAVENGERS,

HYENA-LIKE, DESECRATE THE GRAVES OF THE DEAD PATRIOTS WE REVERE screamed a headline in the Marion, Ohio, *Star*, which denounced Beard and others who thought as he did. But the book exerted an enormous influence on university professors, teachers, and others who were convinced by Beard's argument. Over the next thirty years, Beard's "economic interpretation" found its way into textbooks, popular history books, and school courses, and for a time

The Fourth of July, Nantasket Beach, Massachusetts. Automobiles were a key part of the booming economy of the 1920s.
Courtesy of Culver Pictures, Inc.

became accepted by many as the correct version of how and why the Constitution was drafted.

☞ *We Are Deceived by History*

Charles Beard's impact went beyond his specific arguments. His book made it possible for others to criticize the Founders rather than have to honor them as figures who were perfect and almost superhuman.

In the 1920s, when many writers and journalists were disillusioned with America's "Great Men," this approach to the Founding Fathers became popular. "Debunking," or revealing the selfish motives lurking behind the supposedly public-spirited actions of politicians, business leaders, and clergymen, became a way for writers to express their disgust at the way lies and deception seemed to be taking over the country.

In books and magazine articles, debunkers went after "sacred cows"—people and institutions that were supposedly too important or too serious to be criticized or ridiculed. Some debunkers were angry because bankers and munitions makers, who had encouraged the United States to enter World War I to help "make the world safe for democracy," had used the war to make vast fortunes. And just as government propaganda had duped Americans into thinking the war was being fought for purely high-minded reasons, they claimed, advertising agencies were now exaggerating the virtues of products ranging from vacuum cleaners to automobiles in order to get Americans to spend their money. Others blasted the hypocrisy of Prohibition, which furthered the careers of politicians and gangster "bootleggers" while actually making the consumption of alcohol seem glamorous and exciting to millions of Americans. Wherever they looked, critics and intellectuals saw pompous leaders spouting high-sounding speeches on Democracy, Prohibition, Christianity, and Civilization, while they lined their own pockets or sought to gain power.

Aaron Burr, painted by Gilbert Stuart about 1792. Courtesy of the collections of the New Jersey Historical Society, Newark, New Jersey.

★ A SLOBBERY MASS OF FLUBDUB

Some looked back in American history and claimed that this had always been true. Like D. H. Lawrence, the poet William Carlos Williams expressed his discontent with modern American life by blaming the Founding Fathers for creating a soulless society devoted to money making and a deadening self-control. America after the Revolution had become "Hamiltonia—the land of the company," where huge corporations controlled the American people and where factories polluted the rivers and natural landscape that Williams loved.

But the poet found a hero in the one Founding Father who was condemned by the history books—the dashing and enigmatic Aaron Burr, from Williams's own state, New Jersey. Burr fought bravely as an officer during the Revolution. After the war, he became a lawyer in New York City, a U.S. senator, and then Thomas Jefferson's vice president. But long-simmering animosity between him and Alexander Hamilton led to the duel in which Burr shot and killed Hamilton. After that, Burr became involved in what is still one of the most mysterious and least understood episodes in American history—a plot to lead an expedition of sixty armed men to the West in 1806 for some kind of military conquest.

Whether Burr was aiming to take over part of Mexico from the Spanish Empire or to set up his own independent domain in President Jefferson's Louisiana Purchase territory, as some claimed, will probably never be known. Arrested by American authorities before his expedition could reach its objective, he was put on trial for treason against the United States, but was acquitted because the charge could not be proved. Burr went into voluntary exile in Europe, returning to New York only at the end of his life. He went down in the history books as Hamilton's murderer, a political schemer, and a probable traitor, the "black sheep" among the revolutionary leaders. The fact that his personal life was full of mistresses, prostitutes, and illegitimate children only made matters worse.

Williams saw Burr differently. "In that man there burned a springtime of the soul . . . like a bird in flight," he wrote in his book *In the American Grain,* published in 1925. The Revolution of 1776, Williams argued, had been fought "for the sense of the individual"—to allow each man and woman to find himself or herself, to pursue happiness wherever it might lead, without regard for the opinions and inhibitions of others. But Washington, Hamilton, Franklin, and the other Founders, preoccupied with money and power, betrayed the Revolution by creating a society hemmed in by rules and prejudices that kept individuals from fulfilling themselves. Burr was different; he possessed "a humanity, his own, free and independent, unyielding to the herd." It was true that Burr's sexual escapades proved him to be a "lover of the senses," but Williams applauded this. A *truly* free America would be one where each person, like Burr, might embrace his or her own sexual and spiritual identity. Rather than killing Hamilton in cold blood, Burr had been forced to do it: Hamilton, who resented and envied Burr's "free spirit," had pursued him with hatred until Burr had no other choice.

Instead of being the villain of the early republic, Williams suggested, "this courteous, well-bred, able silent man" had been one of the few revolutionaries who continued to fight for the true freedom of the individual. "We are deceived by history," Williams lamented. "America had a great spirit given to freedom but it was a mean, narrow, provincial place; it was NOT the great liberty-loving country, not at all. Its choice spirits died." Williams turned the history books on their heads to argue that what modern America needed was more Burrs and fewer Hamiltons and Washingtons.

☞ Countries Have No Fathers

George Washington was the favorite target of the debunkers. In 1926, a century and a half after the Declaration of Independence, the "Father of His Country" was the subject of two biographies that scrutinized his life in new and strikingly irreverent ways. William E. Woodward's *George Washington: The Image and the Man* and Rupert Hughes's *George Washington: The Human Being & the Hero* both sought to uncover the "true" Washington by stripping away the layers of myth that surrounded him.

Woodward, a journalist, novelist, and inventor of the word *debunk*, explained that he wrote his biography because he could not stomach the existing books on Washington. In those books, Washington "was depicted as a godlike character who never made a mistake in his life and who was always moved by infinite wisdom, foresight and courage. . . . I could not bring myself to believe that such a person ever really lived." Woodward began by hacking away at the greatest legend of them all: Weems's cherry-tree tale. Woodward showed that the story was "a brazen piece of fiction," and produced evidence that Washington actually told white lies from time to time.

One by one, Woodward deflated other myths. The first president, Woodward insisted, was poorly schooled. The idea passed down in history books that he had attained a high level of education by teaching himself was part of

By showing an adult head on the six-year-old Washington's body, and slaves working in the background, Grant Wood's painting Parson Weems' Fable *(1939) debunks the cherry-tree legend.* Courtesy of the Amon Carter Museum, Fort Worth, Texas.

★ **A SLOBBERY MASS OF FLUBDUB**

"the slobbery mass of flubdub in which he has been submerged so long that it has hardened around him and can be chiselled off in chunks." The legend spread by ministers that Washington had been a deeply religious man, and had knelt in the snow at Valley Forge to pray for God's aid in defeating the British, was also nonsense: "He seemed, according to the evidence, to have had no instinct or feeling for religion. . . . The name of Jesus Christ is not mentioned even once in the vast collection of Washington's published letters."

What was worse, Woodward wrote, Washington was not a particularly likable or even interesting person. Washington was reserved and dull in his social life. He was "the kind of man who doesn't shake hands . . . who has no gossip . . . who listens to your best jokes with a solemn face, and says coolly, 'Is that so?' " As a plantation owner and businessman, he was obsessed with making money, even if it meant mistreating others. Woodward wanted Americans to know that the "Father of His Country" had sold Tom, one of his slaves, away from his home at Mount Vernon to strangers in the West Indies. Washington had informed the ship captain entrusted with the task of selling him that "this fellow is both a rogue and a runaway . . . [but] he is exceedingly healthy, strong, and good at the hoe . . . which gives me reason to hope that he may with your good management sell well, if kept clean and trim'd up a little when offered for sale." Woodward also maintained that Washington had married the widow Martha Custis, "a small, dumpy young woman, with dark eyes and a sharpish nose," not because he loved her, but in order to get her "slathers of money, slaves, land."

Nor was Washington a "Great Man" in the conventional meaning of the phrase. As a general, he had missed his opportunity to create a truly effective guerrilla army, and instead had chosen to fight the British regulars on their own terms. Washington's victory over the English had owed more to luck than to his military ability. As a thinker, "he was entirely devoid of original ideas," and his writings were "a vast Milky Way of hazy thoughts"; he left the hard work of creating the American government to Jefferson, Hamilton, James Madison, and others. All in all, Washington had been a lucky man who managed to be in the right places at the right times. Woodward even denied that

WASHINGTON MEETS NEW ORDEAL

Myths Are Found Still Clinging Round the Father of His Country Despite the Efforts of His Latest Critics to Eradicate Them---Another Statement of the Washington "Problem"

Again the light of research and reappraisal is turned on George Washington. Two recent books have reawakened the discussion, which became active two years ago, as to the real Washington, in contradistinction to the "superman" of myths. In the following article Dr. Dodd, Professor of History at the University of Chicago, seeks to determine to what extent recent efforts have disclosed the true Washington.

By WILLIAM E. DODD

GEORGE WASHINGTON comes into the pillory, his perfumed and powdered locks exposed to the closest scrutiny. Nor does he undergo the ordeal without some singeing; and many good people seem to be worried. There have always been good folk who worried over the appearance of the naked truth in history. They think socialism will prosper, whatever socialism may be. But there is little reason to become uneasy. It was to be expected; the surprise ought to consist in the fact that Washington has not been "exposed" long ago. What is the problem and how has the fame of the revered Founder of the Republic suffered?

The misfortune began with the pious New England purpose to make capital of Washington for their thrifty commercial ventures. A great Virginian stabilizer to neutralize the wild follies of Jefferson and the true Virginians! That was what Alexander Hamilton, Fisher Ames, George Cabot and Oliver Ellsworth sought to do and did for the eight years of Washington's Presidency; and Washington served the purpose so well that he all but wrecked the most popular Administration that was ever set up in these United States, going to his grave almost without a friend in his native State and with only one or two Congressional districts that sent men to Congress who paid any attention whatever to what the great General said: Leven Powell of Loudoun County and John Marshall, who got in on a fluke from the Richmond district. That was a bad end.

Then the Southern slaveholders, the cotton kings of the first half of the nineteenth century, took it into their heads to capitalize Washington, the slaveholder, the exponent of things as they were, abandoning Jefferson and all his foolish works, about 1830, Washington the model exponent of a democratic social philosophy! The disciples of Calhoun united in this with John Marshall and his followers, who delivered the Supreme Court to the desired propaganda. They went the New Englanders one better and even drove them to the arch heretic, Thomas Jefferson, just before the cataclysm of 1861—Lincoln announcing in 1858 that he and the New England Republicans were but Jeffersonians! The Southerners made as bad a mess of their Washington propaganda as Hamilton, Cabot and the other Federalists had done. The Civil War was in the offing.

So much for the political sanctification of the first and perhaps the greatest President. The lying Parson Weems of Maryland started the so-called historical deification in 1802. Then John Marshall, the unfittest of men to wield the historian's pen, published several dull volumes to make good Weems's false story. Although Marshall knew Washington personally he constructed a most untruthful story by adhering strictly to facts. One may build a hideous house of the most beautiful materials. As if that were not enough, Washington Irving entered the field of historical biography just before the opening of the Civil War and published five volumes of a Washington that was better, though not a great deal better, than Marshall or Weems—Irving remembering that the first President had laid his hands in blessing on the head of the young Knickerbocker. How could he draw any but an ideal portrait? Nor was Washington unideal.

But after the deluge of the '60s, the New Englanders took to Washington again, the Southerners hardly in a fit state of mind to reply or even protest. Of all the misleading biographies of Washington, Lodge's is the worst. But Lodge, in his dull, "scholar-in-politics" way, managed to set Washington, till Sidney George Fisher of the pious City of Philadelphia bethought him to try to tell the truth about the American Revolution. He succeeded in a fair way; and Worthington Ford, a new Englander with a difference, in "The True George Washington" blurred Lodge's masterpiece. Then came the incomparable ex-Senator Beveridge in his four volumes of "John Marshall," and through clever side thrusts of his brush put Lodge's picture of Washington back on the centre of the stage—the truths of that epoch, as offered by Beard and Bemis, Alvord and Schlesinger, being buried underneath a magnificent vilification of Jefferson and the "foolish folk" who made the Revolution. Washington, according to the gospel of Saint Henry Cabot, standing there draped in immaculate social robes made in England, his huge feet encased in delicate shoes, his great, bony hands in gloves of fashionable size and his hair all powdered and done up in a perfumed bag, not a false tooth or a pinch of pyorrhea in his head. There we leave for the moment the unfortunate demigod, damned by his friends.

Now comes the (Continued on Page 20)

"Washington Is Not Yet De-Mythed."

★ A SLOBBERY MASS OF FLUBDUB

the first president could really be considered the Father of His Country: "Revolutions and countries have no fathers. They are created by the mass movements of a race; they are the composite results of a thousand separate causes, all woven into a single pattern. . . . Had Washington never lived, the United States would undoubtedly be here to-day."

In his book, Rupert Hughes dwelled on the fact that instead of being the "spotless saint of school-book tradition" or the "dull gray bore manufactured by stupid dullards, stodgy politicians and mongers of untruisms," Washington got angry, liked to gamble, and enjoyed alcohol. "Liquor of all kinds he loved and manufactured, imported, gave away and consumed in vast quantities."

While both Woodward and Hughes clearly wanted to shock their readers, their books caused an angry backlash that surprised even them. William Lanier Washington, a descendant of George's brother Augustine, denounced the books as "very rotten—that is the only word to describe them." One critic blasted the two writers for being "gutter historians," and compared them to "dogs" digging around in the "cemetery" of the nation's heroes. In Wisconsin, the Federation of Women's Clubs passed a resolution "against expressions of disrespect and disloyalty to the great men in our history." Throughout the country, writers and speakers rushed to defend Washington's reputation. When Hughes gave a lecture in New York and mentioned that Washington was so fond of parties and dancing that he had once danced all night long, an elderly woman said loudly, "Well, why shouldn't he? He was the Father of our country!" and stormed angrily out of the hall.

Clergymen and others argued that the debunkers were hurting America by destroying Washington as a role model for children and teenagers. S. Edward Young, a Presbyterian minister, claimed that "if the young men and women of

"Washington Is Not Yet De-Mythed." Writers and professors seeking the "real Washington" scrutinize the larger-than-life Founding Father in this 1926 cartoon from the New York Times Magazine. Courtesy of the New York Times / NYT Pictures.

America were made to believe that Washington was as bad as these present exhibiters of his faults or follies would make him out to be, irreparable damage would be done to the ideals of the oncoming generation. . . . They will be at Lincoln next." Young echoed the views of the conservative veteran's group the American Legion, which warned that a student "led to believe that a great National hero was guilty of weakness and crime" was more likely "to excuse such failings in himself and others."

Everywhere, it seemed, Americans still wanted to see George Washington as a hero, and many of them resented Woodward and Hughes for trying to undermine him. When asked by reporters about the controversy, President Calvin Coolidge—a man of few words—simply smiled, glanced out the White House window, and said, "The monument is still there."

Woodward and Hughes responded to their critics by reasserting that they were presenting the "true" Washington to the public. But they were also willing to admit that George Washington was not all bad. "He was not a man of first-rate ability," Woodward stated, "but in many ways he was a great man." If he lacked imagination and warmth, Washington *was* strong-willed, brave, and persevering. He had the organizational ability and patience to keep the Revolutionary War effort going while the thirteen states withheld troops and funds and their representatives bickered in Congress. "Washington's mind was the *business mind*," Woodward claimed. "There are many Washingtons among us to-day. I know six or seven myself. Such men are usually found in executive positions in large-scale industrial or financial enterprises."

The two authors also pointed out that rather than criticize Washington, their main aim was to show him as a living and breathing human being. Like any person, they argued, Washington had his failings and his problems. He quarreled with his mother. He had terrible dental problems, and by the time he was president wore a set of false teeth that made his mouth look swollen. As a young man, he had fallen in love with Sally Fairfax, the wife of his friend and neighbor, and continued to write her love letters even while he was courting Martha Custis.

"To take such a man," Hughes asserted, "suppress his outbursts of impatience, his mistakes, his foibles, his ignorances, his unwisdoms; to correct his spelling, his grammar, [turning] his whole life into a text-book . . . is not only a hypocritical outrage on truth, but also a heartless disservice to Washington." John Thornton Washington, the president's great-great-grandnephew, agreed with Hughes, admitting that the great man "cussed and drank like a gentleman and made some of the best whiskey in Virginia." "Why try to place a halo around George Washington?" he asked.

To hide Washington's flaws would not only be lying, the debunkers argued; it would actually make it *harder* for young people to identify with him. In the Jazz Age of the 1920s, when sophisticated teenagers were exposed to the temptations of bootleg liquor, smoking, sex, and the freedom from parental control offered by the automobile, the perfect Washington who "chopped down the cherry tree" seemed silly and boring. He was also unrealistic as a role model. As one book reviewer asked, "Does it really spur on the youth of America to imitate George Washington if we endow George with all the superhuman virtues? Isn't the schoolboy of 1926 more likely to throw up his hands in face of that unattainable pattern? By humanizing George Washington, by bringing him near to Bill Smith and Henry Jones, aren't young Bill and Hank encouraged in the useful belief that they, like George, may rise above their human limitations?"

In the end, the debunkers showed that they had mixed feelings about the Founders. On one hand, they enjoyed the thrill of cutting the nation's greatest heroes down to size. Yet they also showed that the revolutionaries had been real human beings, not impossibly perfect statues. By doing so, they reinvented the Founders so that Americans in a new, less reverent age could identify with them—warts and all. It was Washington's flaws that made him interesting, even likable. Rather than detracting from his greatness, his humanity enhanced it.

Debunkers and defenders of Washington continued to argue and accuse one another of misrepresenting the first president. Their jibes at each other were aired in newspapers, radio interviews, and congressional debates. But in 1929, the arguing stopped. Intellectuals and ordinary people were forced abruptly to look at the revolutionary leaders in a different way. Suddenly, Americans needed Founding Fathers and Mothers who could help them withstand the worst economic crisis in the nation's history.

Like the Dark Days of Valley Forge

THE GREAT DEPRESSION AND WORLD WAR II

☞ *The Year of Washington*

"EVERY MAN, WOMAN, AND CHILD—EVERY VILLAGE, TOWN, AND CITY—SHOULD GIVE EXPRESSION OF HOMAGE TO THE FATHER OF OUR COUNTRY DURING THE BICENTENNIAL CELEBRATION IN 1932." So thundered one of the bulletins of the George Washington Bicentennial Commission, a group sponsored by the federal government and entrusted with the task of organizing a massive nationwide celebration of the two hundredth birthday of the first president. The Commission, which included congressmen, professors, teachers, and prominent citizens, labored to make 1932 the Year of Washington. The Commission kept busy distributing "a George Washington Appreciation Course in handbook form" to thousands of teachers, encouraging schools and church groups to put on plays about the Revolution, and publishing sixteen pamphlets on such subjects as "Washington the Farmer" and "Washington the Military Man."

But the Commission planned its festivities against a backdrop of economic disaster. The Great Depression, which had begun in the autumn of 1929, was a blow that seemed to threaten the very survival of American society. By 1932

"The father of his country" inspires the leaders of tomorrow. Norman Rockwell's The Guiding Influence, *painted for the Washington Bicentennial in 1932.* Courtesy of the Norman Rockwell Museum, Stockbridge, Massachusetts.

twelve million Americans—almost one third of the workforce—were jobless. Factories, banks, and stores had shut down across the country. Thousands squatted in makeshift shantytowns, called "Hoovervilles" after President Herbert Hoover, who seemed unable to pull the country out of its crisis. Others lived a hand-to-mouth existence as hoboes drifting back and forth across the country in search of work. The luxuries of the prosperous twenties became distant memories as many Americans struggled to avoid homelessness or even starvation.

Yet millions of Americans responded enthusiastically to the Bicentennial. Towns and organizations from coast to coast mounted Washington pageants and celebrations. Americans of all races and ethnic backgrounds held festivals. When the year was over, the Bicentennial Commission reported that American schools had conducted at least 3,548,292 individual programs to honor Washington.

In the depths of the Depression, Americans needed George Washington. But it was not the flawed man with false teeth revealed by the debunkers whom they wanted. Facing an uncertain and frightening future, many turned to Washington as a model of strength and courage, the kind of heroic leader the United States had to have *now* to pull the country out of economic catastrophe. "The dark cold days of Valley Forge are not far from the bleak and hopeless days of 1932," asserted John Crawford, a winner of a nationwide college oratory contest sponsored by the Commission. "We need today a Washington with an unselfish and courageous conviction . . . a Washington with a far-reaching conception of statesmanship who will work out a righteous solution to the great problem of starvation in a land of plenty."

☞ A New Jefferson

For millions of Americans, the man they elected president that year represented just such a hope for forceful leadership. Franklin Delano Roosevelt entered the White House fully aware of the enormous challenges he and the country faced. A man accustomed to wealth and privilege, he now found himself the leader of a country in which millions were jobless and hungry. But

African–American kindergartners, and Navaho students in Arizona, celebrate George Washington's bicentennial, 1932. Courtesy of Columbia University Libraries.

Roosevelt was a brilliant communicator who knew how to use his personal warmth and charm to reassure and inspire confidence. He had triumphed over catastrophe in his own life, continuing his political career despite the polio that left him paralyzed from the waist down at the age of thirty-nine. An avid reader of American history, F.D.R. was fascinated by the lessons he felt he could learn from the experiences of the Founding Fathers as statesmen. He also shrewdly realized that the American people needed to see a president who was not afraid to be measured against the great leaders of the nation's past. In frightening times, Americans had to hold on to the glories of that past in order to pull together and prevail. Roosevelt did what he could to convince the American people that he was a leader in the mold of heroes long gone but still revered.

In his speeches, press conferences, and radio "fireside chats," Roosevelt often mentioned Andrew Jackson and Abraham Lincoln—two men of the people who had led the nation through turbulent times. But it was about Thomas Jefferson that F.D.R. expressed his strongest feelings. As a lifelong Democrat, it was natural for Roosevelt to pay homage to the man credited with establishing his political party. But his passion for the Virginian went beyond this. In the 1920s, as governor of New York, Roosevelt had been active in the movement to acquire the third president's estate at Monticello, Virginia, for preservation as a national landmark.

Now, as president, he subtly led Americans to see the similarities between himself and the Sage of Monticello without ever making the comparison directly. Jefferson, he noted in a speech, "was a great gentleman. He was a great commoner. The two are not incompatible." The president knew that this statement would make many think of *him*, a man of inherited wealth who yet remained in touch with the problems and dreams of ordinary working people. When Republican newspapers attacked his policies, Roosevelt reminded the public (with some exaggeration) that "against Jefferson were almost all the newspapers and magazines of the day." He directed his aides to compile folders filled with quotations from Jefferson's writings, for use in explaining and justifying his plans to the country.

While running for president, Roosevelt had promised "a new deal for the American people" if elected. In 1933 and the years that followed, he sought to deliver on his pledge. Working with the "New Dealers"—the small army of ambitious reformers, economists, social workers, and lawyers he had brought with him to Washington—Roosevelt pushed a range of bold and sweeping laws through Congress. Federally funded programs like the Civilian Conservation Corps and the Works Progress Administration gave jobs and a regular paycheck to millions of unemployed men and women who became forestry workers in the national parks, builders of roads and bridges, or artists creating murals in post offices and government buildings. Other New Deal programs used government money to control flooding, bring electricity to rural areas, and guarantee high crop prices for farmers.

As never before, the federal government stepped in to regulate the way Americans did business and led their daily lives. Laws established minimum wages and maximum hours in the workplace. The government created a Social Security system that guaranteed financial protection to those out of work due to illness, disability, or old age. Under Roosevelt, the federal government for the first time came out wholeheartedly for the labor movement, backing the right of workers to join unions and bargain with employers for better wages and conditions.

New Dealers proudly announced that this expansion of government embodied the spirit of Thomas Jefferson. Henry Wallace, Roosevelt's secretary of agriculture and later his vice president, maintained that the New Deal was "a twentieth century model of Jefferson's principles of government." In the eyes of Roosevelt and his advisers, Jefferson was the great Apostle of Democracy. He had been the Founding Father most devoted to creating an America where the common man would have an opportunity to rise economically if he was enterprising and worked hard. A nation of independent, self-reliant individuals pursuing their own happiness was Jefferson's recipe for healthy government.

Now the Depression threatened democracy. Joblessness and poverty were shaking the faith of millions in the American system; in despair, people gave up believing that democracy worked. Some sought alternatives in dangerous totalitarian ideologies, such as fascism or communism. By seeking to end the Depression, Roosevelt argued, the New Deal was rescuing Jefferson's America, an America where economic opportunity and representative government went hand in hand.

But the New Dealers went beyond this. The national emergency of the Depression also gave them a chance to enact reforms that they hoped would continue to transform American life even after the economic crisis was over. They worked to create a society where government—by organizing and funding everything from dams and hydroelectric plants to public housing and art exhibits—would offer the great mass of people happier, more secure lives.

Here, again, Thomas Jefferson was their patron saint. After all, Jefferson had sought life, liberty, and the pursuit of happiness for "the people." Now the New Dealers defined "the people" in terms that went far beyond Jefferson's. They often tried to overcome bigotry by making African-Americans, Asian-Americans, Latinos, and Native Americans eligible for work and relief programs. The very poor, whose impact on the country Jefferson feared, were included in New Deal projects. Women, who had won the right to vote in 1920, were also an important force in the New Deal. Eleanor Roosevelt, the president's wife and close adviser, and Frances Perkins, his secretary of labor, were arguably the most politically powerful women in American history up to that point. The New Dealers maintained that they were taking Jefferson's spirit of democracy and, in light of changing times, expanding it to include ever-larger numbers of the American people.

☞ The Real *Jefferson*

"This is a very prosperous time for Thomas Jefferson," a newspaperman named Simeon Strunsky wrote in 1936. "Everybody has a kind word for him. Nearly everybody writes a book about him. Every political party and faction in the end calls him father." Indeed, Roosevelt's love for Jefferson seemed to spread throughout the country. Biographies and magazine articles portrayed the third president as "Tom" Jefferson, the man of the people who liked the feel of the soil under his fingernails. (In reality, Jefferson, an aristocrat born and bred, probably would have viewed as insolent the public use of any version of his first name other than Thomas.) Artists working under New Deal programs adorned the walls of the Library of Congress in Washington with murals celebrating the life of the six-foot redheaded Virginian. In 1938 Congress approved a law placing Jefferson's profile and a view of Monticello on the nickel, just as they had put Washington's head on the quarter six years before.

With the Roosevelt Administration backing passage of the Wagner Act, which guaranteed the right of workers to organize, labor unions also claimed Jefferson as their hero and inspiration. This was especially true where corporations and local governments continued to resist unions. When police arrested nine longshoremen on strike against tankers owned by the Standard Oil Company at docks in Modesto, California, in 1935, a workers' newspaper responded angrily: "Were law abiding citizens such as Jefferson and Lincoln alive today, they would no doubt be rotting in some filthy jail much the same as our brothers at Modesto." After all, in his first Inaugural Address President Jefferson had stated that a good government "shall not take from the mouth of labor the bread it has earned." If government was not supposed to hurt laborers, didn't it follow that government was supposed to help them to win their rights and protect them from greedy employers? Emboldened by federal support, industrial workers proudly wore their union buttons as "badges of a new independence," and compared their strikes to the Boston Tea Party. For these Americans as for others, the decade of the thirties, with its air of crisis and of dramatic new possibilities, truly seemed to be a revolutionary age.

Millions of voters, many of them helped by New Deal programs, loved Franklin Roosevelt. They returned him to office in 1936 and 1940, making him the first president to serve three terms. But other Americans hated and feared him. Many wealthy businessmen, most of them Republicans, saw F.D.R. as "a traitor to his class" who was paying for his expensive relief programs by taxing the rich. They regarded the New Deal as a form of "creeping socialism," which under the guise of ending the Depression was unleashing a horde of meddlesome government bureaucrats on the land, leading to complete government control of the economy, as in Communist Russia.

But the rich were not the only people to oppose Roosevelt. Substantial numbers of Americans, including some members of Roosevelt's own Democratic Party, feared that he was becoming a dictator, drunk with the power that the New Deal had given him. Unlike George Washington, who had established a tradition by refusing to run for a third term in 1796, they saw Roosevelt getting carried away with his immense popularity, which ensured that he would be reelected again and again.

In 1936 Republican businessmen and a small group of prominent Democrats formed the American Liberty League to warn the country about the danger they believed that Roosevelt posed. Addressing a banquet of two thousand Liberty Leaguers in Washington, Al Smith, ex–New York governor and formerly one of Roosevelt's closest Democratic allies, blasted the New Dealers. "It is all right with me if they want to disguise themselves as Norman Thomas [head of the Socialist Party] or Karl Marx, or Lenin, or any of the rest of that bunch, but what I won't stand for is allowing them to march under the banner of Jefferson, Jackson, and [Grover] Cleveland." F.D.R. was a fraud, Smith argued, who was trying to dupe the people into thinking he was a new Jefferson when he was betraying and killing the *true* meaning of Jefferson's message.

The *real* Jefferson, Liberty Leaguers maintained, was the man who had defined "a wise and frugal government" as one "which shall restrain men from injuring one another, which shall leave them otherwise free to regulate their own pursuits of industry and improvement." The true meaning of democracy for Jefferson, they asserted, was a limited government that kept out of the daily life and economic affairs of the people. New Deal regulations and taxes were threatening the liberty of the individual to acquire and enjoy property. The rich should be free to be rich, without interference from governments or labor unions. Sooner or later, Jefferson had believed, too much government, even if well intentioned, became tyranny. This was exactly what was happening under Roosevelt's New Deal. Roosevelt's big-government schemes were, according to Republican Congressman James Beck, "realizing beyond any dream of Alexander Hamilton his ideas as to the nature of our government and what its desired form should be." The only way to protect individual liberty and the pursuit of happiness was strictly to limit government programs and the spending that went with them. *This,* not the New Dealers' reckless bloating of government, was the true spirit of Thomas Jefferson.

A furious F.D.R. responded by attacking the wealthy industrialists and bankers he believed were trying to derail his programs. At the Democratic convention in Philadelphia in June 1936, as he accepted nomination for a second term as president, Roosevelt noted that "political tyranny was wiped out at Philadelphia on July 4, 1776." Washington's and Jefferson's Revolution had overthrown "the eighteenth century royalists who held special privileges from the crown." But a different kind of threat was being posed in 1936 by new enemies of freedom, the president added. "The age of machinery, of railroads; of steam and electricity; the telegraph and the radio; mass production, mass distribution" had given rise to "economic royalists"—wealthy industrialists, bankers, and transportation tycoons—who preyed on the average American in ways "undreamed of by the fathers."

In this and later speeches, Roosevelt sought to show that had he been alive in the 1930s, Jefferson still would have supported the New Deal. While his opponents quoted the Monticello Sage on the virtues of small government, Roosevelt recalled Jefferson's warning that "widespread poverty and concentrated wealth cannot long endure side by side in a democracy." In the twentieth century, only the "organized power of Government" was strong enough to protect the people from the greed of large corporations.

☛ *International Conspiracies*

F.D.R. won the 1936 election against his Republican challenger, Alfred Landon, by a landslide. But while New Dealers and conservatives continued to accuse each other of mangling Thomas Jefferson, others found different and even more controversial meanings in the lives and ideas of the Founders.

As Roosevelt had warned, the crisis of the Depression led some Americans to question the very foundations of the nation's political and economic systems. American Communists lauded developments in the Soviet Union, where the dictator Joseph Stalin was supposedly creating a classless society without poverty or economic instability. Thousands of Americans, hoping that the overthrow of the capitalist system would bring them true security and equality, flocked to the ranks of the Communist Party of the United States of America.

During the 1920s, Communists throughout the world, following the directives issued by Stalin in Moscow, had called for international revolution against capitalism in the United States and elsewhere. In the early days of the New Deal, American Communists rejected Roosevelt's reforms as not going nearly far enough to change the country. Capitalism had created the Depression, and capitalism must go. Radical measures were called for, they argued: The working classes must take over the country's factories, banks, railroads, and farms from capitalists and create a new revolutionary government to control the economy for all the people. The idea that either Democrats or Republicans truly honored the principles of 1776 was a joke. "Never was there such a mass of people so completely deprived of all semblance of 'the right to life, liberty and pursuit of happiness,'" the Communist Party's American manifesto declared. The Communist magazine *New Masses* published a poem that portrayed capitalist bosses and politicians sporting patriotic symbols to conceal their use of lynch mobs and thugs against American workers and racial minority groups:

> *God Flag Constitution*
> *holy trinity of exploitation*
> *signifying American Legion*
> *D.A.R.*
> *Ku Klux Klan*

*with Declaration of Independence
in one hand
and tar and rope in the other.*

But by the mid-1930s, Stalin, alarmed by the rise of Mussolini in Italy and Hitler in Germany, encouraged American Communists to befriend capitalist liberals and persuade them to join in a "Popular Front" against the common enemy, fascism. Earl Browder, the head of the American Communist Party and its presidential candidate in 1936 and 1940, complied. In speeches, interviews, and the pages of the party's newspaper, the *Daily Worker,* he sought to convince the American public that communism was "twentieth century Americanism," a movement as much rooted in domestic political traditions as in the radical ideas of Marx and Lenin.

Again and again, Browder argued that the patriots of 1776 and the Communists of the 1930s believed in the same ideals. He celebrated Thomas Paine for his opposition to conventional religion, which he implied resembled the Communist Party's resistance to religion as "the opiate of the people." He championed Patrick Henry, "whose famous shout, 'As for me, give me liberty or give me death!' re-echoes down the corridors of time." Browder also glorified Jefferson, "whose favorite thought revolved about watering the tree of liberty with the blood of tyrants." American Communists took Browder's message out into the streets. When the conservative Daughters of the American Revolution neglected to celebrate the anniversary of Paul Revere's ride in April 1937, members of the Young Communist League marched through New York City carrying a sign proclaiming "THE DAR FORGETS BUT THE YCL REMEMBERS."

Browder tried to convince Americans that "our American giants of 1776 were the 'international incendiaries' of their day. They inspired revolutions throughout the world. . . . The Declaration of Independence was for that time what the Communist Manifesto is for ours. . . . Revolution was then 'an alien doctrine imported from America' as now it is 'imported from Moscow.' "

While some liberals were willing to work with Communists against international fascism, many Americans—including anti-Soviet leftists—ridiculed Browder's efforts to paint Stalinism in red, white, and blue colors. Charles Yale Harrison, a disgruntled ex-Communist who had become disgusted with the party's dictatorial policies, wrote a satire in which Earl Browder was "disguised as Paul Revere in breeches and a cocked hat." Standing beside his overworked horse, Browder tried to dupe reporters into thinking that Communists "believe in American democracy, in the spirit of the frontier, the covered wagon, Buffalo Bill . . . Casey Jones and other heroic figures in our nation's copybook past."

Communists were not the only radicals agitating for change in America during the Depression years. Across the country, small groups of right-wing extremists also envisioned a "New Order" for the future. Rather than idealizing the Soviet Union, these activists wanted the United States to follow the lead of fascist Italy and Nazi Germany, where totalitarian regimes had supposedly overcome the Depression and eliminated poverty and disorder.

Like the European Nazis they modeled themselves on, these American rightists—organized in small, often semisecret groups with names like the Silver Shirts and the Christian Legion—called for a militaristic dictatorship and blamed Jews, African-Americans, and other minorities for the country's ills. Like the Ku Klux Klan before them and the white supremacists of today, they claimed to represent the true, "racially pure" America that supposedly had been overrun by members of "inferior" racial groups. They despised Roosevelt and claimed that Communists were part of an "international Jewish conspiracy."

In 1934 an obscure magazine called *Liberation*, published in Asheville, North Carolina, ran what it claimed were selections from the private diary of Charles Pinckney, one of the delegates to the Constitutional Convention of 1787. *Liberation* was published by William Dudley Pelley, leader of the Silver Shirts of America. The magazine asserted that Pinckney had recorded in his diary a speech by Benjamin Franklin at the Convention in which Franklin attacked Jews. According to *Liberation*, Franklin had warned his fellow delegates that if they did not write a clause into the Constitution prohibiting Jews from entering the United States, "in less than 200 years they will have swarmed in such great numbers that they will dominate and devour the land and change our form of government. . . . I warn you, gentlemen, if you do not exclude the Jews for all time, your children will curse you in your graves." The Convention, of course, had not written such a prohibition into the Constitution, and Pelley declared that America was now paying the price for not listening to Franklin.

The magazine article was soon reprinted enthusiastically by propaganda sheets in Nazi Germany and by other right-wing periodicals in the United States. Meanwhile, historians took a long and hard look at Pelley's evidence. The alleged diary had never been seen by anybody but Silver Shirts, and no other record of such a speech by Franklin existed; soon it became apparent that the "diary" had been invented by modern anti-Semites. The language attributed to Franklin didn't even make sense. At one point in his "speech," Franklin condemned Jews for being "Asiatics"—a modern racist idea that had not even existed in Franklin's day. Prominent Franklin scholars such as Carl Van Doren and Julian Boyd publicly blasted the entry as a modern forgery. "Not a word have I discovered in Franklin's letters and papers expressing such sentiments against the Jews as are ascribed to him by the Nazis—American and German," noted Charles A. Beard. When Jewish Philadelphians tried to raise money to build a synagogue, Franklin had not only signed their petition appealing for contributions but had also donated five pounds of his own money, as he often did when religious groups needed funds to erect houses of worship. Rather than being able to prove that Franklin had hated Jews, the Silver Shirts ended up discrediting themselves as forgers while their "proof" disappeared into thin air. Today, though, some extremist militia groups have run the old story on the Internet as if it has never been disproven.

Other hate groups besides the Silver Shirts also tried to use the Founding Fathers to prove the "Americanness" of their ideas. While many German-Americans were disgusted by what Adolf Hitler was doing to their ancestral homeland, a group of several thousand calling themselves the German Amer-

American Nazis celebrate Washington's Birthday in New York's Madison Square Garden, February 20, 1939.

ican Bund tried to start an American branch of the Nazi Party. On the evening of February 20, 1939, the Bund held what it called a "Pro-American Rally" to celebrate Washington's birthday in New York City's Madison Square Garden. A crowd of twenty-two thousand, including three thousand uniformed Bund storm troopers, filled the auditorium to hear speakers celebrate the leadership abilities of George Washington and Adolf Hitler. On the walls above them, an array of American flags, swastikas, and banners reading "Stop Jewish Domination of Christian America" flanked a thirty-foot-high portrait of Washington. The country was in bad shape, Bund member G. W. Kunze told the audience, "when Henry Morgenthau [F.D.R.'s treasury secretary, a Jew] takes the place of Alexander Hamilton and Franklin D. Roosevelt the place of a Washington." The nation's problems had begun, Bund leader Fritz Kuhn declared, when the Continental Congress had accepted loans from the Jewish businessman Haym Salomon. Now Roosevelt, a vocal anti-Nazi, and the Jews were turning America into a "Bolshevik paradise." Only Nazism could save

Christian civilization and the "Americanism" of 1776. "The time will come," Kuhn warned, "when no one will stand in our way."

Promising to uphold the Bund members' First Amendment right to free speech, New York's Mayor Fiorello LaGuardia had provided seventeen hundred brawny policemen to protect the Nazis from protesters. "Our government provides for free speech, and in this city that right will be respected. It would be a strange kind of free speech which permits free speech [only] for those we agree with. That's the kind of free speech they have in Fascist countries—but it isn't free speech." Yet the rally enraged many New Yorkers. Thousands of demonstrators, including Jews, African-Americans, and members of veterans' groups, some chanting "keep the Nazis out of New York," surrounded Madison Square Garden on the night of the Bund celebration. Fourteen people (including one man who tried to jump on stage and disrupt Kuhn's speech) were arrested after scuffling with police and Bund members. Anger at the Nazi commemoration of Washington's Birthday spread beyond New York.

In Congress, Representative Martin of Colorado compared the Bundists to "the hired Hessians of the Revolution." The Bundists, he noted, were trying to convince Americans that Nazis believed in Christian and patriotic values when they were actually creating a "pagan dictatorship" in Germany and denouncing Jesus Christ as a "dirty Jew pig." Rather than being a commander of men in the mold of Washington, Adolf Hitler was "the greatest enemy in the world of everything that George Washington stood for, and of everything that America typifies."

Radicals of the left and right were not very successful in their efforts to convince Americans that they had the answers to the problems of the Depression. Their attempts to use the Founding Fathers to prove that their ideas were not alien or dangerous failed to impress more than a minority of the population. Yet the ideologies they represented would shortly be colliding headlong on the battlefields of Europe, at the cost of millions of lives. Americans, too, would soon be shedding blood in combat around the world. At home and abroad, men and women turned to their revolutionary past once again, this time to help them weather the hardships of war.

On October 15, 1939, tens of thousands of people, most of them Polish-Americans, marched up New York's Fifth Avenue to celebrate the birthday of the Revolutionary War hero Casimir Pulaski. But the mood of this, the third annual Pulaski Day parade, was not festive. Most marched in silence and many were in tears. Six weeks earlier, Nazi Germany had launched a surprise attack on Poland and quickly routed the Polish Army. Unknown to the marchers, on that very Sunday Hitler's tanks and storm troopers were obliterating the last resisting Polish regiments. World War II had begun.

Franklin Roosevelt had watched the rise of Adolf Hitler with alarm and, as president, had denounced the Nazi persecution of German democrats, liberals, and Jews. Now he realized that, sooner or later, the United States would have to involve itself in the European war in order to halt the Nazi onslaught. This became urgently clear after the fall of Denmark, Norway, the Low Countries (Belgium, the Netherlands, and Luxembourg), and France to Nazi armies in the spring of 1940 left Britain standing alone against Hitler. Roosevelt knew that most Americans wanted to stay out of a foreign war. He saw that, slowly but surely, he would have to use his powers of persuasion to awaken the country to the threat posed by Nazism around the world.

On December 7, 1941, the Japanese Navy and Air Force launched an attack on the U.S. naval base at Pearl Harbor, Hawaii, that devastated the American Pacific fleet and took the country by surprise. Overnight, Roosevelt had the popular and congressional support for war that he had been working for. Within days, Japan's partners, Italy and Germany, had also declared war on the United States. America was suddenly neck deep in the most destructive war in human history.

As the government mobilized the armed forces and scrambled to organize the nation's vast industrial might for war, the president sought to reassure and inspire the American public, as he had done in the darkest days of the Depression. In a radio speech on December 15, the one hundred fiftieth anniversary of the ratification of the Constitution's Bill of Rights, Roosevelt reviewed the reasons why Americans had to stand up to the Nazi, fascist, and Japanese imperialist attempts to conquer the world. "The truths which were self-evident to Thomas Jefferson . . . were to these men hateful. The rights of life, liberty, and the pursuit of happiness which seemed to the Founders of the Republic, and which seem to us, inalienable, were, to Hitler and his fellows, empty words which they proposed to cancel forever." The Axis powers of Germany, Japan, and Italy were seeking to impose a tyranny worse than that of George III on the continents of Europe and Asia; Americans could not stand by and let it happen.

As young draftees headed for basic training and civilians (including millions of women) flocked into factories and businesses to help the war effort, patriotic symbols and figures from the nation's past appeared everywhere—in government recruitment posters, in magazine ads, in stage plays and movies. The minuteman of Lexington and Concord, clutching his musket as he left his peacetime plow, showed up in store windows and on billboards as the official emblem for the defense bonds that the government sold to the public to help finance the war. One cigarette company ran an ad that presented the conflict as pitting "Thomas Jefferson versus Adolf Schicklgruber" (Hitler's father's original family name).

Once more, the "ethnic" heroes of the Revolution became vivid symbols for millions of Americans. Celebrated in parades and bond drives, the Marquis de Lafayette and Kosciuszko—two foreigners who had helped the United States win its independence—now became icons of the spirit of freedom that lived on in the resistance movements against Nazi occupation in their native France and Poland. American professors gave lectures on such subjects as "Casimir Pulaski, A Soldier of Liberty." When a statue honoring Haym Salomon was dedicated in Chicago eight days after Pearl Harbor, Salomon was already a symbol of the Jewish role in the founding of the republic, and a reminder of the plight of millions of Jews suffering Nazi persecution throughout Europe. For Jewish-Americans, he now came to stand for their eager participation in the war to destroy Nazism forever.

The Roosevelt administration, realizing that a multiethnic, religiously diverse population had to pull together to win the war, encouraged such demon-

Philadelphia broker Haym Salomon (seated), long a symbol of American religious liberty, became an emblem of resistance to Nazism during World War II. The artist, Frank Reilly, used his imagination in depicting the Jewish revolutionary; no portrait of Salomon survived from his lifetime. Courtesy of the Continental Distilling Corporation.

strations of patriotism. Over the radio, the president called for "a national unity that can know no limitations of race or creed or selfish politics." But Roosevelt also wanted to avoid the mistake of World War I, when German-Americans had been humiliated and attacked. Instead, he emphasized the contributions of Italians and Germans to American history, including the Revolution. He reminded Americans that one of Jefferson's friends was Filippo Mazzei, an Italian emigrant whose statement "All men are by nature equally free and independent" had supposedly helped to inspire the language of the Declaration of Independence. Writers for wartime government publications noted that Baron von Steuben and other Germans had fought against tyranny alongside Washington.

Roosevelt hoped to reassure Americans by pointing out that Nazism and fascism were fleeting movements that the war would soon sweep into history's dustbin. The *true* liberty-loving and democratic spirit of the German and Italian peoples, represented by Steuben and Mazzei, would soon return. But Roosevelt had another purpose as well. Millions of German-Americans and Italian-Americans had to be kept loyal to the war effort; beyond that, many of them were Democrats, and the president counted on their votes. By stressing the role played by German and Italian heroes of the Revolution, F.D.R. sought to persuade large numbers of American citizens and voters that their loyalties belonged to their country, not to ancestral homelands dominated by dictators.

"We will not under any threat, or in face of any danger, surrender the guarantees of liberty our forefathers framed for us in the Bill of Rights," the president announced after America's entry into the war. Japanese-Americans soon discovered that they were the glaring exception to this policy. Unlike German-Americans and Italian-Americans, their numbers were small. They were already subject to anti-Asian racism on the West Coast, where most of them lived, and now to wartime hysteria about a possible Japanese invasion of the United States from the Pacific. Unlike any other group, they were presumed to be potential spies and saboteurs simply because of their national origin. In one of the greatest mistakes of his presidency, Roosevelt signed Executive Order

9066, which allowed the U.S. Army to round up Japanese-Americans and move them to ten "relocation centers"—really prison camps—away from the California coast. Over one hundred thousand men, women, and children of Japanese birth or descent, many of them American citizens, found themselves forced out of their homes and businesses and sent to desert camps, all without trial by jury or any of the other rights supposedly guaranteed by the Constitution. While many of their sons in the U.S. Army died fighting bravely in Europe against Nazi dictatorship, internees lost property and opportunities that they never regained after the war. To these Americans, the praise lavished on Jefferson, Washington, Pulaski, Steuben, and other "freedom fighters" sounded hollow indeed.

☛ Jefferson's War

"The fate of a nation was riding that night," the *New York Times* commented on April 19, 1942. The occasion was the one hundred sixty-seventh anniversary of Paul Revere's early-morning ride to alert the Massachusetts countryside that the redcoats were coming. Revere's heroic act, the *Times* asserted, carried an important lesson for wartime America. "Today, at this very hour, this nation faces the greatest peril in its history. Many men of many callings are awake to that peril. Men [and women, the *Times* could have added] behind the lighted windows of giant factories . . . earnest, trained, devoted officers of the services, who plan far into the night in Washington or fight in jungle and desert and icy outpost a world around."

But, the *Times* warned, even as young Americans were fighting and dying around the globe, there were still too many people at home who did not realize how great was the danger to the future of the United States and democracy. "A long time has passed since 1775," the newspaper admitted. "But we can still remember Paul Revere, riding out into the 'hour of darkness and peril and need,' so that the people would 'waken and listen, to hear the hurrying hoofbeats of his steed.' "

Paul Revere's ride seemed urgent in the early months of 1942, for the war was not going well for the United States. The Japanese Army and Navy had defeated American forces in the Philippines and swept triumphantly through Southeast Asia. German U-boats were sinking American ships and with them millions of tons of war supplies, often within sight of the U.S. coastline. While Britain's cities had survived bombardment by the German Air Force, Axis armies now threatened the very survival of Russia and China, America's other principal allies.

On February 23, 1942, Franklin Roosevelt delivered a Washington's Birthday "fireside chat" over the radio. "We have most certainly suffered losses," the president admitted, "from Hitler's U-boats in the Atlantic as well as from the Japanese in the Pacific—and we shall suffer more of them before the turn of the tide." What Americans needed to do was pull together as a nation, face the fact

Safeguarding the "American way of life." The image of the minuteman of Lexington and Concord, used to promote the sale of wartime savings bonds, adorns this World War II Coca-Cola ad. Courtesy of the archives of the Coca-Cola Company.

that victory would not come easily, and work hard to win the war. If they could not do so, the result would be disaster. "If we lose this war," Roosevelt warned, "it will be generations or even centuries before our conception of democracy can live again."

Americans already had a model for how to win the war. "For eight years," Roosevelt recounted, "General Washington and his Continental Army were faced continually with formidable odds and recurring defeats. Supplies and equipment were lacking. In a sense, every winter was a Valley Forge." Still, Washington and his men had struggled on—and triumphed. Americans in

1942 would have to be just as selfless. They would have to accept long work-days, demanding production quotas, and government rationing of everything from gasoline to nylon stockings.

At the same time, Roosevelt added, they would have to endure the taunts of defeatists who would try to undermine their morale. The revolutionary troops had faced similar resistance. "Throughout the thirteen states there existed fifth columnists—and selfish men, jealous men, fearful men, who proclaimed that Washington's cause was hopeless." In response, Washington had turned to the words of Tom Paine, written while the "little army of ragged, rugged men was retreating across New Jersey, having tasted nothing but defeat." Roosevelt recited Paine's words of encouragement: " 'The summer soldier and the sunshine patriot will, in this crisis, shrink from the service of their country; but he that stands it now, deserves the love and thanks of man and woman. Tyranny, like hell, is not easily conquered; yet we have this

Remembering the lesson of Valley Forge. A U.S. government poster issued to stir patriotism during World War II. Courtesy of Library of Congress Poster Collection, Division of Prints and Photographs.

consolation with us, that the harder the sacrifice, the more glorious the triumph.' "

"So spoke Americans in the year 1776," the president concluded. "So speak Americans today!"

Valley Forge quickly became a symbol of the need for self-sacrifice and hard work, and for optimism as well. After U.S. troops invaded North Africa in late 1942, war correspondent Frank Kluckhohn described young American infantrymen, bearded and mud-spattered, marching forward to challenge the German Afrika Corps "through weather almost as cold and certainly as damp as that of Valley Forge." Even after Allied forces successfully landed in German-occupied France, Valley Forge remained a symbol of the hardships that lay ahead before victory could be achieved. On June 18, 1944, twelve days after D day, the Allied invasion of France, on the anniversary of the Continental Army's departure from Valley Forge in 1778, Pennsylvania Governor Edward Martin spoke from the site of Washington's camp to urge Americans to "work harder, talk less and produce more."

While Roosevelt summoned forth images of American boys going shoeless, hungry, and cold during the hard winter of 1777, Thomas Jefferson remained the figure he used most persistently to inspire the American people. He was delighted when Polish diplomats-in-exile noted his physical resemblance to a portrait of Jefferson housed in the Polish embassy in Washington, sketched by the revolutionary hero Tadeusz Kosciuszko. Indeed, declared the journalist Arthur Krock, "except for the eighteenth century hair-do and a difference in the nasal skyline, Kosciuszko's Jefferson bears so striking a resemblance to Franklin D. Roosevelt that the addition of a long cigarette-holder would bring the engraving near the margin of a likeness."

It was Jefferson the advocate of human rights that Roosevelt and his advisers sought to commemorate by building a Jefferson Memorial, to be dedicated on the bicentennial of Jefferson's birth, April 13, 1943. Party politics had been the original driving force behind plans for such a monument. During the New Deal years, when Republicans and Liberty Leaguers were attacking his programs, Roosevelt had noticed that the nation's capital was home to monuments

The same face? Franklin Roosevelt was pleased when people noted his resemblance to this sketch of Jefferson by Tadeusz Kosciuszko (seen here in an aquatint version by Michel Sokolnicki). Left: courtesy of AP/ Wide World Photos. Right: courtesy of the National Portrait Gallery, Smithsonian Institution.

honoring Washington (a Federalist) and Lincoln (a Republican), while the Democrat Jefferson went uncelebrated. "I thought it was sort of a funny thing that one of our three greatest presidents had no memorial in the National Capital—practically no memorial of any kind," he told reporters in 1938.

F.D.R. stopped just short of accusing Republicans of conspiring to prevent a monument from being built because they secretly hated Jefferson's democratic ideas. When Roosevelt announced plans for a Jefferson Memorial and statue to be constructed at the edge of the Washington tidal basin, Republicans *did* cry foul, arguing that the project was simply another New Deal boondoggle really calculated to glorify Roosevelt instead of the Sage of Monticello. One opponent snorted that a Jefferson statue should be erected only if it depicted the third president "with tears streaming down his cheeks" in grief at F.D.R.'s "big government" programs. When Republican newspapers charged that the construction would uproot hundreds of cherry trees lining the basin and diminish the annual influx of tourists who flocked to see them, thus hurting Washington's hotel business, F.D.R. denounced such allegations as "a flim-flam game." "So far as hotel keepers are concerned—well, I am just a hick from Dutchess County, a Democratic hick," a smiling Roosevelt told reporters, "and when I go back to Dutchess County I think it would be quite a magnet to me to come back to Washington, as a tourist, to see this new Jefferson Memorial, with another thousand cherry trees down around that basin." With the coming of war, the purpose of the proposed memorial became to celebrate Jefferson, the Apostle of Liberty.

By the spring of 1943, when Roosevelt presided over the dedication of the completed Jefferson Memorial, the tide of war was turning, as he had predicted. American forces had begun to roll back the Japanese in the Pacific. A joint Allied landing in Sicily and the Italian mainland foreshadowed the D-day invasion of a year later. Hitler's Russian campaign had ground to a standstill at Stalingrad, and the Red Army had begun its counteroffensive to drive the Nazis from Soviet soil. American war production had reached fever pitch, with factories churning out tanks, ships, planes, artillery, ammunition, and supplies to fuel the Allied war effort around the globe. While the New Deal had helped many survive the Depression, the demands of the wartime economy for workers finally brought the return of prosperity. In Europe, Asia, and at home, the dark days of Valley Forge seemed numbered.

Voters chose Roosevelt again in 1944, making him the first and only president to be elected to four terms. But the war had taken its toll on him; by the early months of 1945, he was ill and fatigued. As Allied armies closed in on Berlin, the president prepared an address for Jefferson Day, April 13, 1945. Roosevelt returned to the themes he had struck throughout the war. "Today," he wrote, "this Nation which Jefferson helped so greatly to build is playing a tremendous part in the battle for the rights of man all over the world." But he never delivered the speech. At 4:35 P.M. on the afternoon of April 12, Franklin Roosevelt died at Warm Springs, Georgia. Less than a month later, the German armed forces surrendered, ending the war in Europe. With the Japanese surrender to the United States in August, World War II was over.

Few presidents have left their mark on an entire era as Franklin Roosevelt did. In his twelve years in office, he led the country through two of its greatest crises. F.D.R. and his aides dramatically enlarged the federal government to solve the problems of the Depression, and they transformed the country into a wartime "arsenal of democracy." While doing so, Roosevelt sought to unite Americans by urging them to look backward. He realized that in troubled times, it reassured Americans to find a sure footing on the bedrock of their nation's past. Remembering the Revolution helped people to define for themselves what it meant to be American in an age when political and religious freedoms were being threatened around the world.

But not all Americans agreed with Roosevelt's version of that past. While New Dealers celebrated Thomas Jefferson as the apostle of opportunity and equality for the common man and woman, a visionary who would have welcomed the expansion of government and organized labor in the people's interest, Republicans and conservative Democrats championed a very different Jefferson. Their Jefferson was the defender of individual liberties and the right to be wealthy against the encroachment of big government and big labor. Radicals of the left and right added their own voices to the heated arguments over the true meaning of the Spirit of '76. As they peered and squinted back to Monticello and Valley Forge, Americans of the Roosevelt era began a debate about the meanings of liberty, equality, and the pursuit of happiness that would persist into a postwar era of prosperity and conflict, and ultimately into our own time.

I Call Upon You to Be Maladjusted

PROSPERITY AND PROTEST, FROM THE FIFTIES TO THE VIETNAM WAR

☞ *Everybody Ought to Be Happy Every Day*

"Everybody ought to be happy every day," President Dwight D. Eisenhower advised the American people in the 1950s. "Play hard, have fun doing it, and despise wickedness." Americans enthusiastically followed "Ike's" advice. After the hard times of the Depression and the turbulence of World War II, the postwar years were a time to enjoy the good things that American life had to offer. A booming industrial economy was creating the most prosperous society in the history of the world. With jobs readily available in "white collar" offices and "blue collar" factories, veterans married their sweethearts, bought "dream houses" in the suburbs, and started a baby boom. A comfortable middle-class life was within the grasp of more people than ever before in American history. While Americans bristled at the "wickedness" of an aggressive Soviet Union and worried about the possibility of nuclear war, an endless stream of consumer goods and services—cars, dishwashers, air conditioners, deluxe supermarkets, drive-in movie theaters, televisions—promised a future of continued prosperity and American world leadership.

Not all Americans loved the "fabulous fifties." Nowadays "the bland lead the bland," the economist John Kenneth Galbraith complained in 1958, and "originality is taken to be a mark of instability." In New York and San Francisco, Beat poets and novelists suggested that America was becoming a society of "yes men" afraid to use their imaginations or to be controversial in any way. With so many pursuing the same safe and predictable American Dream, critics worried that individual creativity was being snuffed out. Advertisers held sway over a nation of television-watching consumers whose lives revolved around the latest "new and improved" product.

By the early sixties, Betty Friedan and other writers began to question whether middle-class life was really fulfilling for women, stuck in the house as homemakers while their husbands commuted to work. And the nagging persistence of poverty and racial discrimination raised questions for those prevented from enjoying the Dream. In the late 1950s and 1960s, African-Americans and students launched explosive movements aimed at answering even deeper questions. What did America really stand for? Whose rights and liberties did the Founders' Declaration of Independence and the Bill of Rights protect? And was it possible to win those rights if the nation refused to acknowledge them?

But in the early fifties, millions of Americans didn't care. The decline of controversy and conflict seemed a small price to pay for the pursuit of happiness on the golf course or at the backyard barbecue.

☞ The Wonderful World of America

In the postwar years, many historians as well as advertisers and politicians saw the United States as a society of peaceful, middle-class consumers. Was there something distinctively American, they began to ask, about this prosperity and this lack of conflict? Were these traits rooted in the nation's past? Richard Hofstadter, Louis Hartz, David Potter, and other members of a new generation of college professors believed that they were. These "consensus historians" rejected Charles Beard's idea that conflict between different social classes— farmers and businessmen, workers and industrialists, rich and poor—explained the nation's political history. Instead, they argued, the opposite was true. What was striking was how often political opponents had agreed with each other, how little serious conflict there was between different classes or over different ideas. Yes, the consensus historians admitted, Federalists and anti-Federalists had argued heatedly over the Constitution, and political parties acted as if they were battling each other to the death. But on closer inspection, Federalists and anti-Federalists, Jeffersonians and Hamiltonians,

Pursuing the "American dream"? This Native American, postwar, middle-class family in Martha's Vineyard, Massachusetts, gathers around the television set. Courtesy of AP/ Wide World Photos.

Democrats and Republicans, really agreed with each other on basic values and principles. Jefferson, the so-called radical, and Hamilton, the supposed aristocrat, actually shared slightly different versions of the same vision: Both wanted the United States to be a capitalist republic. So had most Americans throughout the nation's history.

This was possible because, from its colonial beginnings, America had always been a land of "middling" farmers, manufacturers, and merchants. Unlike Europe, with its impoverished peasant masses and wealthy noblemen, early America had few really poor or extremely rich people. While the revolutions of modern Europe had pitted the poor against the rich and radicals against royalists, the American Revolution was an event that allowed a unified population to continue doing what it did best—make money. Even the Northerners and Southerners who had fought the Civil War over slavery agreed when it came to basic political and economic ideas. Following the lead of the Founding Fathers, the United States had become a middle-class society with few dissenters or rebels, a place where even the poor immigrant dreamed of getting his piece of the American pie rather than plotting to overthrow the government.

This new view of the American Revolution and American history became immensely popular. Beard's "economic interpretation" lost its place in textbooks; instead, students read about agreement in a middle-class society. Teachers and readers often overlooked the fact that Hofstadter and Hartz were actually criticizing the consensus, since they felt a lack of opposing viewpoints had blocked creative and honest solutions to the country's problems. Instead, most students learned a different lesson from the new books: The country had always been more or less like the prosperous, placid America of the Eisenhower years. In light of the two world wars and the bloody Communist takeovers that had torn apart Europe and Asia in the twentieth century, the United States looked like an exceptional place, blessed with comparative peace and harmony. The historians' picture of the country's past mirrored the way most Americans wanted to view the nation's present in the 1950s.

When Americans watched television or vacationed, they learned similar lessons about the American Revolution. On television, *Walt Disney Presents* broadcasted the adventures of the dashing South Carolina "swamp fox" Francis Marion while neglecting to explore the part played by Southern blacks who fought on both the American and British sides during the Revolution. The message was the same when families piled into the station wagon for summer vacation. At Mount Vernon, Monticello, Colonial Williamsburg, and other favorite tourist sites, the Revolution seemed to be a struggle planned, fought, and won by ingenious and prosperous white men. Revolutionaries like Crispus Attucks and Deborah Sampson were downplayed or forgotten. During the fifties, most Americans did not hear the voices of the women, the slaves, the Native Americans, the servants, and the laborers who had also made the Revolution and created a new nation.

☞ *The Right to Independent Thought*

"I have here in my hand a list of 205—a list of names that were made known to the Secretary of State as being members of the Communist Party and who nevertheless are still working and shaping policy in the State Department." With this sentence, spoken to the Republican Women's Club of Wheeling, West Virginia, on February 12, 1950, Senator Joseph R. McCarthy launched one of the most notorious political careers in American history. McCarthy's charge that the State Department was riddled with secret Communists and "subversives" seeking to overthrow the government made headlines around the country. The accusation allowed the Wisconsin senator to start a five-year crusade to root out supposed "reds" and their sympathizers working for the U.S. government. McCarthy's Senate subcommittee interrogated scores of federal employees, resulting in the dismissal of many and making him one of the most powerful men in the country.

The only problem was that McCarthy's allegations were based on half-truths, unproven rumors, and outright lies. By bullying, blackmailing, misusing the Senate's rules of procedure, and manipulating the press, McCarthy got away with ruining the careers and reputations of officials whose only real "crime" had been to associate with the "wrong" people, or support liberal causes that the senator deemed subversive. Whenever pressed to provide proof of his accusa-

TV 16183

"WALT DISNEY PRESENTS"
"THE SWAMP FOX"
a TV production for
A. B. C.

tions, McCarthy diverted attention by making even more sensational claims about the number of Communists infiltrating the government—again without producing any evidence. A new word, *McCarthyism,* entered the English language to describe his technique of character assassination and intimidation.

The fifties were ripe for a Joe McCarthy. Following World War II, most Americans viewed the Soviet Union as an evil dictatorship bent on controlling the rest of the world. The Communist menace seemed to surface everywhere. An atomic arms race between the United States and Russia, the Communist takeover of China, and American involvement in the Korean War fanned fears that the country was vulnerable to Communist traitors. In an era when the Soviet Union used spies to obtain American nuclear weapons secrets, the fact that some individuals drawn to communism during the Depression now held influential government positions was alarming. These people became the subjects of suspicion, even though most had abandoned communism years before. Democrats and Republicans both played on the fear, forcing government employees to undergo "loyalty" interrogations and starting congressional committees to investigate alleged Communist infiltration of universities, Hollywood, and the television industry. McCarthy, hungry for power and publicity, merely followed the pack.

McCarthy thrived on fear—not only fear of communism, but also the anxiety of decent people who realized that if they dared to challenge him they might become his next targets. Even influential members of McCarthy's own Republican Party felt it was too risky to criticize him openly. "The other senators were now afraid to speak their minds, to take issue with him," noted Margaret Chase Smith, Republican of Maine, the only woman in the Senate. "It got to the point where some of us refused to be seen with people he disapproved of." Journalists thought twice about writing their honest opinions for fear of attracting the senator's attention, and people removed "controversial" books from their shelves.

Walt Disney Presents *featured the actor Leslie Nielsen as Frances Marion, the Swamp Fox, in its television series on the revolutionary hero.* Courtesy of the Walt Disney Publishing Group. Copyright the Walt Disney Company.

Smith, however, had the courage to oppose McCarthy. She drafted a Declaration of Conscience, signed by six other senators, which asserted that his methods violated the basic liberties the Founding Fathers had written into the Bill of Rights. "Those of us who shout the loudest about Americanism," she insisted, "are all too frequently those who, by their own words and acts, ignore some of the basic principles of Americanism." Among those principles were "The right to criticize; The right to hold unpopular beliefs; The right to protest; The right of independent thought." "Freedom of speech is not what it used to be in America," Smith concluded. "It has been so abused by some that it has not been exercised by others."

People in America and around the world joined Smith in opposing the Wisconsin senator's dictatorial ways. "If by some misfortune you were to quote with approval some remark by Jefferson you would probably lose your job and find yourself behind bars," commented the British philosopher Bertrand Russell. "The Age of Accusation" had come to America, noted William S. White, Capitol Hill correspondent for the *New York Times*: "The square, massive, sad memorial to Abraham Lincoln, the rounded, softer, and more pleasing pile that commemorates Thomas Jefferson—physically these remain, white and cold and lifeless." Certainly, the Jefferson who had proclaimed that "a little rebellion now and then is a good thing" sounded exactly like the kind of radical "subversive" McCarthy was trying to purge from American life.

One group of McCarthy's critics took this idea a step further by making a record album. Produced beyond the senator's reach, in Canada, by anonymous writers and actors, *The Investigator* was bought and sold in the United States "under the counter" as an act of protest. It was one of the first albums of political humor, a genre that would become popular in the sixties.

The script of *The Investigator* was pointed in its satire. On the album, an unnamed senator—clearly meant to be McCarthy—is killed in a plane crash. He wangles his way into heaven, where, aided by Cotton Mather of the Salem witch-hunts, he forms a committee to interrogate "heretics, dissenters, and rebels, many of them with prison records," who are "undermining our way of life." The committee summons Socrates, Voltaire, Martin Luther, Beethoven, and Galileo to explain their "dangerous" views to the committee. One by one, McCarthy accuses each suspect of being a secret agent of Satan, and has them exiled to hell. The committee proceeds to interrogate its next witness:

The Investigator. A fictionalized Senator Joe McCarthy interrogates Socrates, John Milton, Thomas Jefferson, Galileo, and Ralph Waldo Emerson. Record album courtesy of the author.

McCARTHY: *All right, please state your full name.*
WITNESS: *Thomas Jefferson.*
McCARTHY: *Your occupation?*
WITNESS: *President.*
McCARTHY: *Ehh, did you engage in any other occupation, Mr. Jefferson?*
WITNESS: *I was a gentleman farmer.*
McCARTHY: *I'm not referring to that. Is it not a fact that you were an active revolutionary . . . one of the leaders of a movement which had as its aim the overthrow of established government by force and violence?*
WITNESS: *Mr. Chairman, when in the course of human events it becomes necessary for one people to dissolve the political bands which have connected them with another—*
McCARTHY: *C'mon now, Tom, you know you're stalling. Just answer the question. You don't have to make a speech.*

After noting that Jefferson once wrote that "the tree of liberty must be refreshed from time to time with the blood of patriots and tyrants," McCarthy deports him to hell too. McCarthy then makes a big mistake. With power going to his head, he decides to investigate "The Chief" (God), who responds by banishing McCarthy himself to hell. But Satan, complaining that Jefferson and the other "crackpot reformers" are calling for a Congress, refuses to take him. At the album's end, God and Satan agree that the only way to get Mc-Carthy out of their hair is to send him back to planet Earth.

The lesson of *The Investigator* was clear. McCarthyism had created a climate of fear that was eroding the freedom of thought and speech—even for those voicing radical or unpopular opinions—championed by Jefferson and the framers of the Bill of Rights. Individuals would hold back from expressing an original or daring idea, from becoming the next Voltaire or Galileo or Jefferson, for fear of being labeled a subversive and losing their careers at the hands of inquisitors.

In real life, McCarthy's conservative defenders, such as William F. Buckley, Jr., and L. Brent Bozell, argued that his name calling, while unsavory, was part of a tried-and-true American tradition. The senator, they maintained, shouldn't be singled out for criticism. After all, hadn't an angry Thomas Paine once called George Washington a hypocrite? Hadn't opponents called Jefferson "an atheist, an adulterer and a robber," and Lincoln "the baboon president, a low-bred, obscene clown"? McCarthy, they claimed, was merely enjoying his own right to free speech, as did plenty of liberals and left-wingers. What they left out was that McCarthy was using his power to ruin the careers of numerous innocent people.

In the end, McCarthy's actions began to resemble those in the album script. To keep himself in the public eye, his targets got bigger and bigger, his accusations wilder and wilder. Finally, in 1954, he accused the U.S. Army of "coddling" Communists in its ranks. The Senate hearings where he confronted Army dignitaries were televised, and millions of viewers got to watch him badger witnesses and make groundless accusations. McCarthy self-destructed in front of the television cameras. By December, when the Senate voted to censure him, his power was broken.

Yet McCarthy still knew how to attract attention and gain publicity. In 1955 he announced that his years as an anti-Communist crusader had been a tremendous mistake. Now, it seemed, he saw the light: The right to hold unpopular, even antigovernment, views was part of America's precious Constitutional heritage. McCarthy claimed that "he had been reading Thomas Jefferson for the past two weeks and that Jefferson had influenced him in this direction." But he also admitted to one reporter that he was making this statement in order to get into the headlines again. It didn't work. He died two years later.

☞ All *Men Are Created Equal*

The fifties were not merely a decade of conformity to the middle-class American Dream or the demands of McCarthyism. Those who had been denied access to the Dream began to demand their rightful share in it. African-Americans challenged all Americans to take a hard look at what their nation truly stood for, to search their souls and ask whether the promises of the Founders had been fulfilled. "I call upon you to be maladjusted," the Reverend Dr. Martin Luther King, Jr., told an auditorium packed with college students at Berkeley, California, in June 1957. "As maladjusted as Abraham Lincoln who had the vision to see that this nation could not exist half slave and half free. As maladjusted as Jefferson, who in the midst of an age amazingly adjusted to slavery could cry out, 'All men are created equal and are endowed by their Creator with certain inalienable rights and that among these are life, liberty and the pursuit of happiness.' As maladjusted as Jesus of Nazareth who dreamed a dream of the fatherhood of God and the brotherhood of man."

By the time he made that speech, King was already world famous as the leader of the boycott that had forced the city government of Montgomery, Alabama, to desegregate its buses. The nonviolent movement for black civil rights, spearheaded by King and the Southern Christian Leadership Conference (S.C.L.C.), was spreading throughout the "Jim Crow" South. On into the 1960s, black and white clergymen, teachers, students, workers, and families would launch scores of nonviolent demonstrations against discrimination and racism: lunch counter sit-ins in North Carolina; store boycotts and mass marches in Birmingham, Alabama; voter registration drives in Mississippi; campaigns to integrate schools and college campuses throughout the South. In the eyes of many, both friends and enemies of the movement, these attempts to end a century of second-class citizenship for African-Americans seemed like a second American Revolution.

King and other black leaders turned repeatedly to the promise held forth by the Founding Fathers. "In a sense we've come to our nation's capital to cash a check," King asserted in his most famous speech, delivered before a crowd of almost a quarter million people at the Lincoln Memorial on August 28, 1963, during the "March on Washington for Jobs and Freedom." "When the architects of our republic wrote the magnificent words of the Constitution and the Declaration of Independence, they were signing a promissory note to which every American was to fall heir. This note was the promise that all men, yes, black men as well as white men, would be guaranteed the unalienable rights of life, liberty, and the pursuit of happiness." But, King insisted, "instead of honoring this sacred obligation, America has given the Negro people a bad check; a check which has come back marked 'insufficient funds.'"

Indeed, civil rights activists argued, the Founding Fathers themselves had not always fully understood the nature of the promise they were making. "I know that the Declaration of Independence was not meant for me," Benjamin Mays, one of King's early mentors in Atlanta, Georgia, admitted, "that its chief architect, Thomas Jefferson, was a slave owner; . . . that the 'land of the free' and 'sweet land of liberty' are not equally applicable to black and white."

Yet history showed that Americans had always needed to struggle to make the Declaration real and meaningful. "We are experiencing the climax of the continuing social revolution in the United States which began with our Declaration of Independence and our war to throw off colonial rule," the Reverend Ralph Abernathy asserted. "The present struggle is in the best American tradition." After all, King reminded Americans, the Founding Fathers themselves had not believed in giving the vote to poor men or to women. "We see that the poor men of 1776 did not accept disenfranchisement without protest. In a legal manner, these pioneers fought as hard for the vote as they had fought as minutemen at Lexington and Concord. Later when women decided the time had come for them to vote, they were far from submissive or silent. They cried out in the halls of government. They agitated in their homes. They protested in the streets. And they were jailed. But they pressed on."

Civil rights workers, however, paid a price for their struggle. White segregationists, including state and local officials, fought to preserve the system of racial discrimination that had governed the Southern way of life since Reconstruction. Southern whites also compared the civil rights movement to the American Revolution, but their version was starkly different from King's and Abernathy's. Georgia Governor Herman Talmadge, who strove to prevent integration of the schools and public facilities in his state, told whites to seek inspiration from the fortitude of those great Southerners George Washington, Thomas Jefferson, and Patrick Henry. "It will take courage . . . of the kind our forefathers showed when they signed the Declaration of Independence, the kind of courage they showed at Valley Forge, . . . at Gettysburg, and during the Reconstruction Era after the War Between the States."

For many whites in the South, the civil rights movement was not merely an insurrection launched by irresponsible blacks and "outside agitators," but an assault on Southern institutions by the federal government. The Supreme Court's 1954 decision to desegregate schools, as well as actions by Presidents Eisenhower and John F. Kennedy to uphold that decision and protect civil rights activists, led many Southern whites to believe that Northern liberals were using the federal government to destroy the right of individual states to govern themselves. The Ku Klux Klan and other secret racist groups viewed the movement as a call to arms. The real liberties at stake, they claimed, were those of white-controlled Southern states threatened by federal officials as tyrannical as George III. "Remember the Patriots of Valley Forge, Yorktown, Trenton and the Alamo . . . Iwo Jima and Korea," the Klan announced in a pamphlet distributed in Alabama. "Have Thousands Died in Vain For Our Cherished Freedoms? They Have Not." The black and white victims of bombings, kidnappings, and brutal lynchings proved that such racists meant to be taken seriously.

☞ *Liberty or Death*

On July 2, 1964, in the name of all freedom fighters "from the Minutemen at Concord to the soldiers in Vietnam," President Lyndon Johnson signed the federal Civil Rights Act into law. The Act outlawed racial segregation and discrimination in public accommodations ranging from restaurants to gas stations to hospitals, and prohibited unequal access to voter registration. To Martin Luther King, Jr., and millions of blacks and whites throughout the country, the Act represented the most important legislative event since Lincoln's Emancipation Proclamation, even if much hard work remained to be done. But while a century of segregation was beginning to end in the South, the movement for African-American rights was taking another direction in the North. The long, hot summer of 1965 saw the outbreak of violent, destructive riots in Los Angeles's Watts and other major cities. The poverty, discrimination, and despair of the Northern inner cities was sparking a backlash more explosive than the nonviolent movement that had swept through Southern communities.

"For the twenty million of us in America who are of African descent, it is not an American dream; it's an American nightmare," Malcolm X declared in 1964. Angry, articulate, vowing to uphold the rights of black Americans "by any means necessary," including force of arms, Malcolm rather than King became the model for many young black militants in the mid- and late 1960s. As a leading spokesman for the Nation of Islam, also known as the Black Muslims, Malcolm rejected the S.C.L.C.'s vision of a "beloved community" of blacks and whites working together for justice and brotherhood. The Black Muslims turned white racism on its head. In their view, whites were inferior but devious "blue-eyed devils" who had managed to enslave and exploit millions of Africans. Now it was time for Afro-Americans to be proud of their own culture and create their own separate institutions, not integrate themselves into an evil and hateful white America.

Whites had always been the enemy, Malcolm charged in speeches and articles; history proved it. "Our people didn't go to America on the *Queen Mary,* we didn't go by Pan American, and we didn't go to America on the *Mayflower,*" Malcolm told an audience at the University of Ghana during a trip to Africa in 1964. "We went in slave ships, we went in chains." Black Americans had to reeducate themselves; they had been duped by white teachers, textbook writers, and politicians. "When I see some poor old brainwashed Negroes—you mention Thomas Jefferson and George Washington and Patrick Henry, they just swoon, you know, with patriotism. But they don't realize that in the sight of George Washington, you were a sack of molasses, a sack of potatoes." By owning slaves and accepting slavery, the "so-called founding fathers" had been "crooks." (In 1995, when Louis Farrakhan, another leader of the Nation of Islam, addressed the Million Man March he had organized, he described Washington and Jefferson in very similar ways.)

To liberate themselves, Malcolm maintained, black Americans had to reject the lie that the Founding Fathers had established the United States as a free and equal society for all people regardless of color. "The truth is that the Revolutionary War was fought on American soil to free the American white man from the English white man." Like Frederick Douglass a century earlier, Malcolm argued that "it is sheer ignorance, insanity, for our people to celebrate the Fourth of July as Independence Day, while white America denies us the first-class citizenship that goes with independence."

But rather than rejecting the Declaration's false promise of equality and fighting back against racial injustice, Malcolm warned, too many black people were embracing the nonviolent, "wishy-washy love-thy-enemy approach" advocated by King. This, too, reflected a long tradition of black submission. "Not only Crispus Attucks, but many of us in America have died defending America. We defend our master. We're the most violent soldiers America has when she sends us to Korea or to the South Pacific or to Saigon, but when our mothers and our own property are being attacked we're nonviolent. Crispus Attucks laid down his life for America, but would he have laid down his life to stop the white man in America from enslaving Black people?"

Malcolm admired one trait of the Founding Fathers, and one only: their willingness to launch a violent Revolution to win their rights. Unlike Martin Luther King, who preached nonviolent resistance to injustice, Americans in 1776 "didn't turn the other cheek to the British. No, they had an old man named Patrick Henry. . . . I never heard them refer to him as an advocate of violence; they say he's one of the Founding Fathers, because he had sense to say, 'Liberty or death!' " Today, Malcolm added, black Americans were "reaching the point now where they are ready to tell the Man no matter what the odds are against them, no matter what the cost is, it's liberty or death."

Malcolm's message tapped the rage of young urban blacks who felt nothing in common with the privileged white society around them. For these Americans, new laws promising justice were not enough; the time to be patient in the face of racism, inferior schools, meager job opportunities, and poverty was over. Many who did not share Malcolm's Muslim religious beliefs did embrace his commitment to violent confrontation in the name of "Black Power." In the late 1960s, new, militant groups like the Black Panthers created black self-help organizations in the inner cities and challenged the racism of white police and officials. Their angry rejection of white America and its heroes was as stark and uncompromising as Malcolm's. The militant Eldridge Cleaver ignored the Founding Fathers when he looked "with roving eyes" for more radical role models, "for a new John Brown, Eugene Debs, a blacker-meaner-keener Malcolm X, . . . an American Lenin, Fidel, a Mao-Mao, A MAO MAO, A MAO MAO, A MAO MAO . . ."

Other black activists were not so quick to brush aside the African-American fighters of the Revolution. Both Malcolm and King agreed that school textbooks neglected the contributions of black men and women to American history. If African-Americans were to take pride in their own heritage and create their own institutions, then they needed to rediscover black history. In 1968 activists and elected officials in the large black community of Newark, New Jersey, started an annual tradition by celebrating Crispus Attucks Day in March, much like the abolitionists who had honored Attucks over a century before. Twenty-five thousand people marched through

Marchers in Newark parade past City Hall, honoring Crispus Attucks and remembering the Revolution. Courtesy of New Jersey Newsphotos.

Newark's streets, proudly remembering black heroes and carrying banners that insisted, "I Am An American."

Whether celebrated or scorned, the Founders remained alive for black activists. Even though the patriots of 1776 had created a nation divided by racial injustice, they had also been the first freedom fighters, America's homegrown radicals and troublemakers. In the movement for civil rights, their example was hard to escape.

☞ *A Time of Extremism*

"You're living at a time of extremism, a time of revolution, a time when there's got to be a change," Malcolm X told students at England's Oxford University in December 1964, a few weeks before he was assassinated in New York City. "People in power have misused it, and now there has to be a change and a better world has to be built, and the only way it's going to be built is with extreme methods."

Malcolm's message found a receptive audience among young people of all colors in the America of the 1960s. On college campuses and in high schools throughout the country, students inspired by the civil rights movement and black militancy organized to shake up a society they viewed as unjust, undemocratic, and shackled by outdated ideas. For many white students, the "safe," middle-class America of their childhoods seemed narrow and unsatisfying, a place where shiny new cars and suburban houses were valued more than free speech and daring ideas. Exciting things were happening in the world—not only in black communities at home, but also in Africa, Asia, and Latin America, where "freedom fighters" were seeking self-determination by rebelling against European colonial rulers and dictators backed by the U.S. government and American corporations.

Many students turned to the writings of the Columbia University sociology professor C. Wright Mills to understand the America of the early 1960s. If black leaders looked at the American Dream from the outside, Mills spoke for those who felt smothered by it from the inside. Mills complained that the independent, self-reliant American of Jefferson's time was extinct. In his or her place stood a passive consumer, "bored at work and restless at play," whose actions, thoughts, and feelings were shaped by a new ruling class of corporate businessmen, advertisers, Pentagon officials, and government bureaucrats. Rather than grappling with the vital issues of the day in face-to-face debate with their neighbors, as people had done at the time of the Revolution, modern Americans digested prepackaged news broadcasts, ads, and government press releases that told them what to believe and how to behave and vote. True democracy was dead in America, Mills argued. No longer could an independent thinker like Mills's hero Tom Paine stir the populace to take radical action in pursuit of freedom. The networks, radio stations, newspapers, magazines, and book publishers—themselves part of the business "Establishment"—would drown out a latter-day Paine and keep him from reaching a wide audience. The modern mass media, moreover, distracted Americans from thinking seriously about political problems. While George Washington had relaxed with books of philosophy and political theory by Voltaire and Locke, "Eisenhower read cowboy tales and detective stories."

The solution was for intellectuals and young people to reject the "military-industrial complex" running the country. Students could create an alternative America where genuine criticism, debate, and political action for change would be possible. The young men and women who established Students for a Democratic Society (S.D.S.) in 1960 believed that they could change the country through direct action and "participatory democracy." Sharon Jeffrey of S.D.S. explained that " 'participatory' meant involved in decisions. And I definitely wanted to be involved in decisions that were going to affect *me*! How could I let anyone make a decision about me that I wasn't involved in?"

S.D.S. members read a wide range of radical manifestos to understand the revolutions that were sweeping the world in the sixties. Their reading lists included the communist writings of Karl Marx, articles by Cuba's Fidel Castro, and Mohandas Gandhi's theory of nonviolent resistance. But they also read the Declaration of Independence and explored "Jefferson's attitudes on liberty." Young people debating, protesting, and demonstrating in the streets of Boston and Philadelphia had created the United States in the first place. Now, by mobilizing the residents of poor urban neighborhoods to fight for their fair share of city budgets and social services, the S.D.S. and other student groups could revive the nation's democratic promise.

The Vietnam War ignited the student movement of the 1960s. In June 1968 the *New York Times* reported that official U.S. involvement in the conflict between South and North Vietnam had now lasted six and a half years, surpassing the length of America's previous longest war—the American Revolution. By that year, the S.D.S. and other student-activist groups had organized hundreds of protest marches, rallies, and sit-ins against what they saw as an unjust war that was killing tens of thousands of young Americans as well as Vietnamese. While Lyndon Johnson and then President Richard Nixon continued to defend the war as part of the struggle against communism, "New Left" student groups became increasingly confrontational in their antiwar protests. The peace and quiet of the "dull" fifties had been shattered forever.

The sixties were one of the most turbulent decades in American history. The assassinations of John F. Kennedy, Malcolm X, Martin Luther King, and Robert Kennedy seemed to usher in an era of political violence and instability. The war split the country apart, pitting antiwar "doves" against prowar "hawks."

Updating the "spirit of '76." College students lead an anti–Vietnam War march in Boston.
Reprinted with permission of the Pilgrim Press.

Noting that young people and their parents seemed to think and live in separate worlds, newscasters began to talk about a troubling "generation gap." Some students burned their draft cards or dodged the draft by fleeing to Canada, acts unthinkable to the generation of middle-aged Americans who had fought World War II and the Korean War.

Just as alarming, a "counterculture" of young long-haired hippies and yippies, committed to sexual freedom and the use of mind-altering drugs like marijuana and LSD, challenged the very values governing their parents' "uptight" lives. Older Americans were shocked by the "unladylike" behavior of young feminists who burned their bras in rebellion against sexism and demanded equality for women at home and in the workplace. "Don't Trust Anyone Over Thirty" and "Do Your Own Thing," declared the buttons worn by student activists and hippies. Like Malcolm X, many young whites found little to respect in American history, which seemed to consist of the oppression of blacks, Native Americans, Latinos, Asians (at home and abroad), women, and the poor. Patriotic reverence for George Washington or Thomas Jefferson was part of the older generation's shallow and hypocritical world.

"Long hairs" and "crew cuts" clashed violently at a number of antiwar demonstrations, and Chicago police clubbed yippies outside the 1968 Democratic Convention. The stage was set for another confrontation on the Fourth of July, 1970, when the hotel magnate J. Willard Marriott, the comedian Bob Hope, and the Reverend Billy Graham—all friends of President Nixon—organized an "Honor America Day" celebration to be held at the Lincoln Memorial and the Washington Monument in the nation's capital. Although supposedly a "nonpolitical" event, the celebration aimed to bring out the prowar conservatives who Nixon applauded as the "Silent Majority" of "forgotten Americans, the nonshouters, the nondemonstrators."

Indeed, most of the 350,000 people who showed up for "Honor America Day" were members of "middle-class families who supported old-fashioned faith in God and country." "We don't want the United States torn apart," insisted Marriott, who hoped the day would "unify us fundamentally in our belief in our wonderful nation." But the yippies, who had chosen Washington as

"Give Me Liberty Or Give Me Death!" Pro–Vietnam War marchers quote Patrick Henry to defend the draft. Reprinted with permission of the Pilgrim Press.

the site of their own Independence Day rally—a marijuana "smoke-in"—had other ideas. Yippie spokesman Rennie Davis warned that there might be violence, since the Honor America organizers had not submitted to a list of yippie demands, which included "painting the Washington Monument in all the colors of the rainbow to symbolize more unity than only shades of red, white and blue." As Kate Smith opened the festivities by singing "God Bless America," yippies started chanting "One, two, three, four, we don't want your ———

★ I CALL UPON YOU TO BE MALADJUSTED

war." When yippies unfurled a Vietcong flag, they were jeered by young men in blue jeans and crew cuts (proving that not everyone under thirty approved of the "New Left"); fistfights broke out. While President Nixon sent a message thanking the crowd for celebrating "the living spirit of the Fourth of July . . . a spirit that created a free and strong and prosperous nation," police fired tear gas and scuffled with yippie demonstrators, twenty-four of whom they arrested.

Not all protesters thumbed their noses at patriotic traditions, as the yippies did. Some summoned memories of the Revolution to remind Americans that they had the right to protest. Antiwar activists staged rallies on the town green at Lexington, Massachusetts, site of the minutemen's stand against the redcoats, and marched the route of Paul Revere's midnight ride. In New York City in 1967, a group called Veterans and Reservists to End the War in Vietnam dressed up in Revolutionary War uniforms and paraded on Washington's Birthday. "Then and Now: Washington—The President Who Could Not Tell a Lie. Johnson—The President Who Cannot Tell the Truth," their banners declared. Three years later, other New York demonstrators staged a new "Boston Tea Party" by burning a facsimile of a federal income-tax form and urging Americans to stop paying taxes that supported the war.

Such agitation was summed up in a skit on the Smothers Brothers' comedy show, one of the "hippest" and most youth-oriented television programs of the sixties. In the skit, a young, long-haired George Washington is scolded by his parents for going out to a demonstration against the British, where he criticizes King George by shouting "Down with L.B.G." (a pun on L.B.J., President Lyndon Johnson's initials). Rather than being a challenge to the American way of life, such humor argued, free speech and protest was the essence of American patriotism. The skit suggested that if Washington were alive in the 1960s, he might join in the struggle against the Establishment, just as he had done in 1775.

Many older Americans—and some young ones—viewed the protest movements of the sixties not only as a shattering of the peace and quiet of the fifties, but as a rejection of the patriotism and respect that had made America great. Groups like the yippies confirmed their fears by trying to disrupt the Establish-

Dressed in Revolutionary War uniforms, Veterans and Reservists to End the War in Vietnam march next to New York's Central Park on Washington's Birthday, 1967. Courtesy of the New York Times/ NYT Pictures.

ment in every way possible. But some advocates of radical change found themselves turning to the Founding Fathers as role models, even as they fought to bestow rights on groups of Americans the Founders had ignored or rejected. To civil rights workers, black militants, and student activists, extremists and troublemakers like Thomas Paine, Crispus Attucks, and Patrick Henry remained relevant after almost two centuries. The pull of the Revolution—the first mass protest movement in American history—was too strong to be resisted.

The Spirit of '76?

FROM WATERGATE TO THE REAGAN REVOLUTION—AND BEYOND

☞ *Nixon Edition*

> *"What's good for the President is good for America."*
> *"When you have a weak argument, abuse and accuse."*
> *"The thoughts of youth are bad, bad thoughts."*
> *"Thou shalt not be found out."*

These sayings ran in the *New York Times* on October 21, 1970. They were part of "Poor Richard's Almanack—Nixon Edition," a satire by the columnist James Reston aimed at the president of the United States. In order to criticize Richard Nixon, Reston rewrote the lines first penned by "Poor Richard," also known as Benjamin Franklin. But while Franklin had used his "almanack" to teach readers that "a penny saved is a penny earned" and "one to-day is worth two to-morrows," Reston's purpose was to denounce Nixon's deviousness and his stubborn insistence on continuing a bloody overseas war that many felt was unjust and unwinnable. The quality of America's political leadership, Reston's comparison suggested, had certainly taken a turn for the worse since Franklin's day.

Less than four years later, facing impeachment by Congress, Nixon would become the only man ever to resign the presidency. By that time, the Watergate crisis had led large numbers of Americans to share Reston's anger at a president they nicknamed "Tricky Dick." Watergate shook the faith of millions in their government and raised questions that still trouble Americans today. Can we trust politicians? Do they deserve our confidence and admiration? If political leaders lie or use government to serve themselves rather than the people, do the Declaration of Independence and the Constitution really matter anymore? And do the revolutionaries who wrote those documents over two hundred years ago still matter? Does anybody care?

Those questions have been answered in a variety of ways since Nixon's day. The Founding Fathers seem to surface whenever Americans debate the meanings of racial and sexual equality, the rights of individuals to control their own lives, the threat of "big government," and other issues that matter to them. The Founders pop up at strange times in unpredictable ways, as if they are always lurking just around the corner, waiting for the outbreak of the next heated argument.

☞ *The Jefferson Rule*

As the country's thirty-seventh president, Richard M. Nixon scored some impressive successes, including opening diplomatic relations with Communist China. But Nixon's obsession with discrediting those he saw as his political enemies ultimately led him to destroy his own presidency. Enraged by the opposition of student antiwar groups and by the criticism of the "liberal" press, Nixon surrounded himself with a small group of advisers and staffers who were willing to break the law to keep him in power. Facing what was arguably the gravest Constitutional crisis since the Civil War, both Nixon's allies and foes turned to the Founding Fathers for guidance and justification.

Watergate was born in an atmosphere of distrust and hatred that dated to the early months of Nixon's presidency. On April 30, 1970, Nixon escalated the Vietnam War by ordering American troops to invade Cambodia. In response, thousands of students launched antiwar demonstrations on college campuses across the country; the president publicly denounced them as "bums." When National Guardsmen gunned down and killed four students during an antiwar protest at Kent State University in Ohio on May 4, Nixon received a warning from his own secretary of the interior, Walter Hickel.

In a letter sent to the White House, Hickel, himself the father of two college students, maintained that the president was dangerously out of touch with the nation's young people. Hickel compared the situation with that of the thirteen colonies two hundred years before, which had endured "violent protest by its youth—men such as Patrick Henry, Thomas Jefferson, [James] Madison and [James] Monroe, to name a few. Their protests fell on deaf ears, and finally led to war. The outcome is history. My point is, if we read history, it clearly shows that youth in its protest must be heard."

After the private letter was leaked to the press, Hickel admitted that he had asked an aide to look up the ages of these four Founders before he wrote; three were in their twenties when their revolutionary activities began, while Monroe had been a teenager. (Hickel omitted mention of such older men as George Washington and Samuel Adams.) While Hickel left out of the final draft his warning that the Revolutionary War had been "England's Cambodia," he did caution the president to avoid the mistake Britain had made by ignoring the grievances of its colonists: "We have an obligation as leaders to communicate with our youth and listen to their ideas and problems."

Nixon didn't listen. His paranoia about his liberal and radical "enemies" persisted, especially as he prepared to run for reelection in 1972. But then his presidency started to unravel. In the early-morning hours of June 17, 1972, five burglars were caught breaking into the headquarters of the Democratic National Committee in the Watergate office complex in Washington. The five men were apparently there to steal documents and install secret wiretaps. Dogged investigations by Bob Woodward and Carl Bernstein, two reporters for the *Washington Post,* revealed that the burglars had ties to the White House. It also became clear that the White House was trying to cover up its involvement in the break-in.

Slowly, journalists and congressional investigators began to piece together a story that seemed incredible: Aides close to the president had conspired to smear prominent Democrats and liberals by breaking into their offices and stealing confidential papers, planting lies about their private lives, and playing a whole range of illegal "dirty tricks." The White House even compiled a secret "enemies list" of those Nixon hated or feared, a list that included Paul Newman, Bill Cosby, Barbra Streisand, James Reston, Senator Edward Kennedy, ex-Interior Secretary Walter Hickel (who had resigned), and dozens of others.

Despite the gathering evidence of wrongdoing, Nixon won reelection in November 1972. But by the summer of 1973, as a Senate Watergate Committee and a special prosecutor summoned witnesses, the pressing question remained: Had the cover-up originated with White House staffers who had spun out of control, or was the president himself involved? A clear answer seemed possible. All conversations and phone calls between Nixon and his assistants had been tape recorded in the Oval Office. The "Watergate tapes" would surely reveal how much the president knew about what his men were up to.

Yet when Special Prosecutor Archibald Cox subpoenaed the tapes, Nixon refused to release them, or to give testimony before a grand jury. Nixon's lawyers argued that forcing him to disclose private conversations would threaten "the continued existence of the presidency as a functioning institution." The Constitution gave little guidance on the issue, so Nixon turned to history to justify his action. "Every president since George Washington," he announced in a press conference, "has tried to protect the confidentiality of presidential conversations."

He also cited what he called "the Jefferson rule." When Vice President Aaron Burr had been tried for treason against the United States in Richmond, Virginia, in 1807, his lawyers took the unusual step of subpoenaing President Jefferson. Burr argued that confidential documents sent to Jefferson by James Wilkinson, one of his accusers, were crucial to his defense. Nixon maintained that Jefferson had refused to comply with a subpoena to hand over the documents to the court. Instead, Jefferson had provided only his own edited summary of the documents—much as Nixon wanted to do with the Watergate tapes. Thus, Nixon maintained, one of the greatest Founding Fathers had started a tradition of "executive privilege" that permitted presidents to keep

Nixon crossing the Delaware. Basing his drawing on Emanuel Leutze's 1851 painting of George Washington, cartoonist Edward Sorel showed President Nixon and his aides navigating their boat over the bodies of anti-war demonstrators. Courtesy of Barry Schwartz. Used by permission of Ira D. Rothfeld.

sensitive documents and conversations out of the hands of courts and the press.

But historians quickly challenged Nixon's position. George Washington's Pulitzer Prize–winning biographer James Thomas Flexner pointed out that the Father of His Country had allowed a full disclosure of letters when his Secretary of State Edmund Randolph was accused by political enemies of being a French agent. Washington encouraged Randolph "to publish, without reserve, any and every private and confidential letter I ever wrote you; nay more: every word I have ever uttered in your presence." Jefferson scholar

Dumas Malone argued that Nixon had gotten the facts wrong about the 1807 Burr trial: Rather than providing a mere summary of the documents in question, the third president had actually cooperated with the court by providing the evidence it demanded. Yes, Jefferson may have resented the court's demands; unlike Nixon, he complied. The upshot, Malone insisted, was a ringing endorsement by John Marshall, the judge in Burr's trial, of the idea "that the president was subject to subpoena, just like any other citizen."

As newspaper columnists and television reporters grew more and more critical of Nixon's "stonewalling," some Americans steadfastly defended him. In September 1973, a group called the National Citizens' Committee for Fairness to the Presidency published an open letter to Nixon's daughter Julie as an ad in newspapers throughout the country. "Dear Julie," the letter read, "You must have felt more than once like exploding with indignation at the purveyors of political pornography who are gnawing at your father and tearing at the very fabric of our nation."

Rabbi Baruch Korff, the committee's chairman, proceeded to note that Washington, Jefferson, Lincoln, and their families had all suffered at the hands of critics, much as Nixon was being lambasted by the *Washington Post,* the *New York Times,* and CBS and NBC news. "Jefferson's daughter, Martha, must have buried her head in her pillow when reading of her father's disgust with the 'malignant passions of politics and party hatreds . . .' And yet, my dear Julie, time served to elevate Thomas Jefferson to 'one of the loftiest pinnacles in American history,' and so time, too, will raise your father in the eyes of his countrymen to great heights; and, by the grace of God, during his lifetime."

Such historical examples failed to impress members of Congress, who began to press for Nixon's impeachment. In the spring of 1974, the Supreme Court compelled Nixon to turn over the Watergate tapes to Special Prosecutor Leon Jaworski. The tapes revealed that in the days following the Watergate arrests, Nixon himself had obstructed justice by attempting to block an F.B.I. investigation into the break-in. With impeachment almost certain, Richard Nixon resigned the presidency on August 9, 1974, vowing to the end that he was "not a crook."

The lesson of Watergate to some was that the system worked. As long as Americans held on to their Constitution, nobody—not even the president—could break the law. On the Fourth of July, 1973, as the crisis deepened, *New York Times* columnist Anthony Lewis felt the need to remind readers that the country had once produced great leaders. "It is a good time now, if a little painful, to think about Jefferson. He was such an extraordinary embodiment of the qualities that once characterized the leaders of the United States and made possible our independence: disdain for wealth and show, respect for learning, faith in the ultimate power of reason if left unfettered by myth or privilege." As depressing as it was to think how far the presidency had fallen since Jefferson's day, Lewis had a more positive message, too: The people and the press could check corruption if they remained ever vigilant in defense of liberty, as Jefferson had insisted.

But many Americans took another lesson from Watergate. The crisis seemed to prove that Washington was a place where politicians lied, cheated, robbed, and lusted after power, all at the people's expense. In his novel *Burr*, published at the height of Watergate in 1973, Gore Vidal argued that it had always been that way.

Like William Carlos Williams almost fifty years earlier, Vidal sought to debunk the most illustrious Founders by making a hero out of the "black sheep" Aaron Burr. In the novel, an elderly Burr narrates his version of the events of the Revolution and the early republic. Burr's depiction of his colleagues is, to say the least, unflattering. George Washington is dull and pompous. Hamilton hypocritically claims to oppose dueling on principle, but when challenged by Burr, the former secretary of the treasury fires first. And Jefferson invents "brilliant" contraptions that don't really work, like a bed that is supposed to fold into the wall but keeps crashing to the floor. What they all share is a lust for power and a talent for concealing their true motives from the American people. "Odd how Jefferson is now thought of as a sort of genius," Vidal has Burr reflect. "It is true he did a great number of things, from playing the fiddle to building houses to inventing dumb-waiters, but the truth is that he never did any one thing particularly well—except of course the pursuit of power."

If you want to understand Watergate, Vidal seemed to be saying, then understand what the Founding Fathers were really like. Where Anthony Lewis saw in Jefferson an honest, upright "anti-Nixon" for Americans to hold on to, Vidal saw an eighteenth-century version of Nixon himself. All of American history was about politicians fooling voters and textbook writers into thinking they were selfless and great men. Washington, Jefferson, Hamilton, and Madison, who had started this con game, were no better or worse than anybody else. Nixon and his aides, Vidal implied, were simply by-products of this venerable tradition. Future historians would probably end up glamorizing Nixon just as they had glorified the men of 1776. Whether readers agreed with Vidal that Watergate fit perfectly into American history, or with Lewis that Watergate disgraced it, many began to lose faith in the system of government the Founders had created.

☞ *The Buycentennial*

On July 4, 1976, the United States celebrated its two hundredth birthday. A government-sponsored Bicentennial Commission, along with state and local governments, organizations, and businesses, sponsored festivities in virtually every community. Six million people swarmed over the docks of New York Harbor to watch a regatta of two hundred sailing ships from all over the world. One million (including President Gerald Ford, who had pardoned his predecessor Richard Nixon) observed the anniversary in Philadelphia, the city where independence had been declared. Vice President Nelson Rockefeller, country singer Johnny Cash, and actor Telly Savalas led a parade through Washington, D.C., past a crowd of a half million. West Germany sent a museum exhibit on the role of the Hessians in American history. On a tour of the former colonies, Queen Elizabeth of England presented to the American people a "Bicentennial Bell" cast by the same London foundry that had manufactured the Liberty Bell. She also presented a check for $1.80 to the historical society of Weare, New Hampshire, whose farmers had been fined that amount for taking wood from "the King's Forest" there in 1772.

Individual Americans celebrated the birthday in their own ways. While thousands watched an official reenactment of George Washington crossing the Delaware and the Battle of Trenton, livestock breeder Howard Harris, Jr., drove fifty-one cows across New Jersey in a re-creation of General "Mad Anthony" Wayne's 1778 cattle drive to supply Washington's troops at Valley Forge. In Sheboygan, Wisconsin, people gathered on a hillside to throw 1,776 Frisbees. A restaurant owner in Wooster, Ohio, constructed a thirteen-foot-long platform to hold a 5,058-pound blueberry ice-cream sundae decorated with red, white, and blue whipped cream, hundreds of flags, and a banner declaring "God Bless America."

As if to prove that the spirit of the sixties wasn't dead, demonstrators staged counter-bicentennials. Thirty thousand gathered in Philadelphia's Fairmount Park, site of the 1876 celebration, to protest what they saw as the country's continued failure to live up to its promise to provide liberty and equality for all. Advocates of independence for Puerto Rico demanded "A Bicentennial Without Colonies." Karen de Crow, president of the feminist National Organization of Women, read the speech with which Susan B. Anthony had disrupted the Centennial ceremonies in 1876, to symbolize how little progress toward economic and political equality American women had made in a hundred years. But the most eloquent protest came from those who, like Frederick Douglass and Malcolm X before them, refused to observe the birthday at all. "Instead of celebrating on July Fourth I'll be crying, and why shouldn't I?" asked Corbett Sundown, a chief of the Seneca Indian tribe in upstate New York. "What did they do except massacre us? They took all our resources, all our lands, all our game." Hugh Weigel, another Seneca, added, "I would do anything for my country, but I wouldn't cheer the people who took everything away from me."

Others expressed discontent in more humorous ways. In Salt Lake City, a tongue-in-cheek "parade" featured marching bands playing kazoos, a Bicentennial garbage truck, and a motorcycle-riding George Washington. Many Americans couldn't take the Bicentennial festivities seriously. After all, what exactly were they celebrating? A war in Vietnam that had torn the country apart and resulted in defeat after the loss of fifty-eight thousand American lives? A Watergate scandal that made most people think twice about trusting their political leaders? The sense of national purpose, the pride in being American that had brought people together at the Philadelphia Exposition one hundred years before, now seemed to be missing. Many would have agreed with the comments of a West German magazine: "The land that brought us blue jeans, the computer, 'Bonanza,' jazz and drive-in churches . . . now delivers only bad news: a murder rate that doubled within a few years, cities that are dying financially; . . . companies that would not shy at trying to bribe the Pope if that could increase sales."

Government officials and businessmen hoping for tourists' dollars were disappointed by what they felt was a low turnout for the Bicentennial. But the writer Alfred Kazin pointed out that many Americans were turned off by "the 'selling' of the Bicentennial by dumb politicians and inflated media performers."

Using patriotism and the Founding Fathers to make a buck—through Washington's Birthday sales and pictures of the revolutionaries in advertisements—was a tried-and-true American tradition. But the Bicentennial year brought new highs (or lows) in commercialism, with images of George Washington, Thomas Jefferson, Sam Adams, and Paul Revere used to sell everything from cars and dry cleaning to soda and toilet paper.

Jesse Lemisch, a historian at the State University of New York at Buffalo, set his students to collecting such "Bicentennial schlock" (from the Yiddish word for cheap, beat-up merchandise). The whole Bicentennial year, Lemisch concluded, saw "American history Disneyfied and cartoonified," a fact proven by the mass production of schlock. "This stuff kills genuine sentiment. . . . It almost seems, emotionally speaking, as if there were no Bicentennial at all."

In the wake of Vietnam, Watergate, and the "selling of the Bicentennial" in 1976, millions found the Founding Fathers meaningless and a bit boring. In the land of the Almighty Dollar, the nation's past heroes seemed to be little more than faces on the money people carried in their wallets and pocketbooks.

★ ★ ★ ★ ★ ★ ★

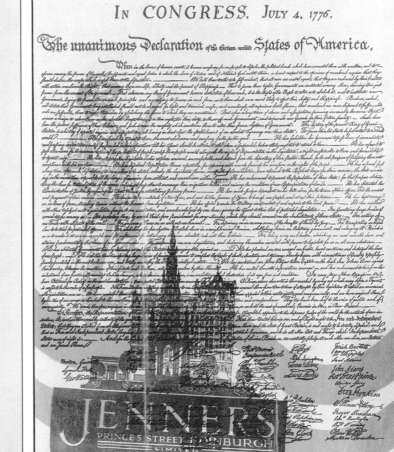

Bicentennial schlock. The nation's two hundredth birthday is used to sell Sanibags, beer, and paper products, 1976.

☞ A New History

Even as the letdown of the Bicentennial made the Founders seem remote and irrelevant, some Americans were finding fresh meaning in the American Revolution. A new generation of historians tried to make sense of the events of the Revolution in terms of their own experiences. As students in high school, college, or graduate school during the 1960s and early 1970s, these scholars were shaped by the protest movements of their own times—the student radicalism of S.D.S., the struggles for black civil rights and against the Vietnam War, campaigns by Mexican-American farm workers and Native Americans for economic and political justice, and the emerging women's liberation and gay rights movements.

To these young men and women, the argument by "consensus" historians that America had always been a conflict-free society whose players were almost always propertied white men just didn't make sense. After finishing graduate school at Princeton University in 1966, Gary Nash moved to Los Angeles, where he took a job teaching history at U.C.L.A. and got involved in the civil rights movement. "My students were far more diverse than in the East," Nash discovered, "diverse in terms of race, class, sex, age, and cultural background. . . . I realized that in my own study I had passed over important aspects of the American past and that these areas of historical concern were often the ones most relevant to the lives of my students."

Young scholars began to rewrite American history "from the ground up." Many described themselves as New Left historians, reflecting their debt to Marxism and other radical philosophies. Some, less comfortable with being typecast as radicals, settled for the label revisionist, meaning that they were revising the interpretations of earlier generations of historians. New Leftists and revisionists scoured archives and libraries for letters, diaries, newspaper articles, tax and census records—anything that might reveal how common people thought, felt, and acted during the American Revolution.

Like William Nell and Elizabeth Ellet more than a century earlier, they rediscovered a whole range of Founding Fathers and Mothers who had been left out of the history books. In studying women during the revolutionary era, Linda Kerber found Nonhelema (also known as Catherine the Grenadier), a Native American who helped save hungry American troops under siege at Fort Randolph on the Ohio River by driving forty-eight head of cattle into their stockade.

According to the research of John Shy and Alfred Young, the Revolution was a war fought and won in large part by the poorest Americans. Some, like the unsuccessful shoemaker and fisherman George Robert Twelves Hewes, who was active at the Boston Massacre and Tea Party and served during the War, were deeply involved in the patriot cause. But others, like "Long Bill" Scott, Zaccheus Brooks, and Joseph Henderson of Peterborough, New Hampshire, were poor artisans, laborers, and drifters who joined and stayed in the Continental Army because they needed the pay and security that military life provided. It was these men who served the longest stints in the patriot armies, sticking by Washington at Valley Forge and winning the war largely because they had failed to make a go of anything else. By uncovering forgotten Founders like Scott and Brooks, historians presented a fresh view of the Revolution—one that was less heroic and more complex than traditional views of gallant patriots rushing to enlist, aflame with the spirit of liberty. It was also a view that reflected the young historians' sense of their own time, a time in which the Vietnam War was fought overwhelmingly by the poor and the undereducated.

The common people—artisans, apprentices, sailors, slaves and free blacks, servants, tenant farmers, farm wives—who sustained the Revolution fought for reasons very different from those of wealthy patriot leaders, the new historians argued. For the humble and the poor, liberty meant opportunity to escape poverty, not merely freedom from British taxes; equality meant the right to vote and not to be treated as inferiors by rich "gentlemen." Many ordinary revolutionaries, imbued with the ideas of Thomas Paine and other pamphleteers, resented the arrogance of the powerful merchants and lawyers who claimed to lead the patriot movement. Women and blacks would have to wait decades for their equality to be recognized. Yet if the Revolution did not live up to all its democratic promises, it did start a radical tradition that lived on in the efforts of labor unionists, abolitionists, feminists, civil rights workers, and antiwar activists to expand the meaning of liberty and equality in America.

The assertions of the New Left historians did not remain unchallenged. A rival group of historians, led by Bernard Bailyn of Harvard, argued just as passionately that the Revolution had been a unifying event that brought together colonists of all identities—rich and poor, merchants, farmers, artisans, and laborers, men and women—in common opposition to British policy. Conflict between underprivileged and elite Americans, Bailyn and his followers maintained, simply was not a crucial issue at the time of the Revolution. Today the two groups continue to argue and debate the true meaning of the Revolution, and the ways it shaped the new nation.

☞ *Intimate Stories*

At the same time that scholars were discovering new Founders among the common men and women of eighteenth-century America, they also rediscovered the "great men" of the Revolution as human beings who led rich and complex emotional lives. In the wake of misleading ads, Watergate, and lies by the C.I.A. and Pentagon, Americans had trouble believing what officials in Washington wanted them to believe. Americans wanted the truth from their politicians, both present and past—including their private thoughts and feelings.

In trying to satisfy such curiosity, a history professor named Fawn Brodie caused a sensation in 1974 when she wrote the best-selling biography *Thomas Jefferson: An Intimate History.*

Brodie asserted that the third president was a man of great passion and sexual energy. Previous biographers, she claimed, did not want to face this aspect of Jefferson's personality because it upset their belief that "Jefferson was a man whose heart was always rigidly controlled by his head; it destroys their image of the supreme man of reason." The problem with this traditional view, Brodie claimed, was that it presented Jefferson as "something less than a man."

What made Brodie's book truly controversial was her willingness to believe James Callender, the journalist who had accused Jefferson of fathering several children by Sally Hemings, a slave. Most historians had dismissed this story as a piece of vicious political propaganda dating back to Jefferson's years as president. But Brodie claimed that the evidence was too strong to be ignored. Even the president's grandson Thomas Jefferson Randolph recalled that one of Sally's sons, when seen "at some distance or in the dusk . . . might have been mistaken for Mr. Jefferson."

Rather than use the Sally Hemings story to blast Jefferson as a hypocrite, Brodie wanted readers to understand and sympathize with Jefferson's dilemma. Jefferson truly loved Sally, she maintained. But the blight of slavery and racism kept him from being able to admit his love to family, friends, and the nation. Had he freed Sally, Virginia law would have forced the ex-slave to leave the state. So instead, he kept her as his property at Monticello and refused to answer the allegations of his political enemies. "The fault . . . lay not in Jefferson but in the society which condemned him to secrecy." In this way, Brodie insisted, the failure of Jefferson and the revolutionary generation to end the horrors of slavery ultimately stunted his private life as well.

Reviewers immediately attacked Brodie's book, triggering a heated debate that continues to this day. The Jefferson scholar Dumas Malone argued that Brodie's evidence was flimsy. Indeed, one of Jefferson's nephews, Peter Carr, had confessed that he and his brother were the true fathers of Sally's children. Other reviewers jumped to Brodie's defense. Older white male historians who disliked the book, they argued, didn't want to let go of their image of Jefferson as a perfect hero without any skeletons in his closet. Some of Brodie's defenders went further, intimating that her "uptight" critics couldn't handle the idea that their hero could love a black woman. The one thing readers could agree on was that Brodie had struck a nerve with her portrait of a man grappling with his sexuality and the human realities of slavery. Exactly who this man was, and what his life meant, remained questions that caused Americans to debate and argue. "After all," commented the writer Alfred Kazin, "Thomas Jefferson is a great part of what we mean by 'America.' "

If the alleged love affair of Thomas Jefferson and Sally Hemings caused Americans to argue and criticize each other, the love affair of John and Abigail Adams gave them pleasure. The Broadway musical *1776*, which opened in 1969 and was later turned into a film, spotlighted their relationship. In 1975 L. H. Butterfield, Marc Friedlaender, and Mary-Jo Kline published a collection of their letters, *The Book of Abigail and John*. The book was followed a year later by a PBS dramatic series, *The Adams Chronicles*, which also depicted the domestic life of the second president and his wife. As in Jefferson's case, readers and viewers were tantalized by glimpses of the private lives of people usually encountered only in textbooks or on marble pedestals.

In the 1970s when the American divorce rate was escalating, the fifty-four-year love affair of Abigail and John Adams seemed as reassuring as a soap opera. Yet Abigail and John had been real individuals, with real emotions and problems. John Adams was the most impatient, high-strung, cranky, and vain of the leading revolutionaries. But he understood his shortcomings and knew that his wife played a major part in helping him to keep his balance. "You shall polish and refine my sentiments of Life and Manners, banish all the unsocial and ill natured Particles in my Composition," he wrote to her shortly before their wedding in 1764.

For her part, Abigail Adams knew that her husband relied heavily on her patience, confidence, and advice during his entire public career. While it was John Adams who had been one of the moving spirits behind the Declaration of Independence, as well as the first vice president and second president, many Americans in the 1970s found Abigail Adams the more intriguing of the two.

In an era when women were supposed to leave politics to men, Abigail played an active role in the Revolution. Like her close friend Mercy Otis Warren—and like many of the lesser-known women discovered by New Left historians—she was immersed in the revolutionary movement. She read and thought independently, often making decisions on important issues before her husband did. "We cannot be happy without being free," she wrote to Mercy Warren. ". . . We know too well the blessings of freedom, to tamely resign it." In her private letters she advocated American independence in the fall of 1775, months before most of the colonies' male leaders reached the same con-

Abigail Adams became a hero to feminists during the 1970s. Adams is believed to be the subject of this 1785 portrait by Mather Brown. Courtesy of the New York State Historical Association, Cooperstown, New York.

clusion. She also was an early opponent of slavery, shrewdly noting that the "passion for Liberty" professed by Virginians was hard to take seriously, since they "have been accustomed to deprive their fellow Creatures of theirs."

But it was her advocacy of women's rights that made her exceptional. In a letter to her husband in the Continental Congress three months before independence was declared, she asked him—and the assembled delegates—to "Remember the Ladies, and be more generous and favorable to them than your ancestors. Do not put such unlimited power into the hand of the Husbands. . . . If particular care and attention is not paid to the Ladies we are determined to foment a Rebellion, and will not hold ourselves bound by any Laws in which we have no voice, or Representation." Abigail's playful threat did not mask the seriousness of her concern.

But John chose not to take her "saucy" letter too seriously. In reply, he hoped "General Washington, and all our brave Heroes would fight" to put down a female rebellion. Unable to vote or hold office herself, Abigail Adams remained her husband's most intimate political adviser through his career as revolutionary and president. No wonder that feminists in the 1970s, fighting for an Equal Rights Amendment to the Constitution and political and professional equality for women, embraced Abigail Adams as a "foremother" and role model.

By writing about Jefferson's sex life and Abigail Adams's political views, the lives of "Long Bill" Scott and Catherine the Grenadier, historians were trying to understand the Revolution in a way that was fresher and somehow truer than what they themselves had been taught in school. Just as the turbulent 1960s and 1970s had taught Americans to "distrust the political speech, the official statement, the news release, the televised press conference," as the editors of *The Book of Abigail and John* put it, they were also tired of "dead Presidents" and statues of lifeless heroes. In reality, the revolutionaries had been complicated human beings with their own sex drives, emotions, and problems; their private lives influenced their public actions. Who were the Founding Fathers? When confronted by a past worth thinking and arguing about, Americans still took the time to struggle with answers to the question.

The election of Ronald Reagan to the presidency in 1980 ushered in a conservative "revolution" aimed at ending fifty years of massive government spending, taxation, and welfare programs dating back to Franklin Roosevelt's New Deal. Like F.D.R.'s foes in the Liberty League, Reagan liked to quote Thomas Jefferson on the dangers of big government. With the president's approval, right-wing Republicans also attacked gay rights, premarital sex, abortion, and other legacies of the "sexual revolution" of the 1960s.

Conservatives were especially angry at the Supreme Court, whose justices had changed American life by ruling in the case of *Roe* v. *Wade* in 1973 that abortion was a right protected under the Constitution. The Court had also ruled that a Constitutional right to personal privacy allowed consenting adults to use contraceptives. Reagan vowed to do all in his power to change the direction of the Court and appoint federal judges who would restore traditional "family values" as the guiding principles of American law. A major opportunity came in 1987, when the president nominated the conservative Robert Bork to fill a vacancy on the Supreme Court. Bork's candidacy immediately sparked an emotional nationwide debate about the Constitution and how the Founding Fathers had meant it to be interpreted.

Bork argued that the Supreme Court had acted wrongly in ruling that the Bill of Rights protected the right of women to have an abortion. Justices, Bork insisted, had concocted a new right of privacy to allow for abortions. No mention of privacy—or, for that matter, of abortion or anything to do with sexuality or reproduction—existed in the Bill of Rights written in 1789 by James Madison and ratified by three quarters of the states in 1791. Madison had drafted clear amendments with language that was understood by the ratifiers. The problem was that modern liberals were trying to twist and distort that language to promote rights the Founding Fathers had never thought about protecting.

By misreading the Constitution, Bork stated, liberals claimed legal protection not only for abortion but also for birth control, gay rights, and other parts

GEORGE WASHINGTON CARVER CROSSING THE DELAWARE

★ THE SPIRIT OF '76?

of their political agenda. Madison and his colleagues had written the First Amendment to protect freedom of speech, not "freedom of expression" for nude dancing, as some liberals maintained. In the same way, liberal justices tried to find room for privacy and abortion in the Ninth Amendment, which guaranteed that rights not listed in the other amendments were still protected. This, too, Bork thought was unacceptable. If Madison had wanted judges to invent new rights out of thin air, he would have written that idea clearly into the Ninth Amendment; but he had not.

The Bill of Rights as penned by Madison, Bork argued, enacted "timeless principles for a free society." When liberal justices distorted their original meaning, they threatened the very existence of democracy in America. The fact that the framers had not dealt with questions of abortion or sex in the Constitution meant that "entire ranges of problems and issues are placed off-limits for judges." Instead, such issues were the business of representatives in state legislatures and Congress. When justices made up new Constitutional rights for abortion or sexual privacy, they took the power to decide such issues out of the hands of the people's elected lawmakers, where such power belonged. Bork admitted that conservatives as well as liberals could unfairly distort the Founders' "original intent" or "original understanding" of the Constitution. For example, he agreed with many on the left that the Second Amendment protected "a well regulated militia," not an unlimited right of individuals to own guns. But his main message was that decades of liberal Supreme Court decisions were wrong and should be overturned.

Many conservatives championed Bork and his idea that the Founders'

The Revolution continues to be reinterpreted and revisualized. Pictures by Robert Colescott and Peter Saul, both based on Leutze's famous painting, demand that we look at the past in new and unsettling ways. Some African-Americans were angered by Colescott's George Washington Carver Crossing the Delaware, *1976, which mixed heroes and stereotypes in a celebration of black "founding fathers and mothers." Saul's* George Washington Crossing the Delaware, *1975, offered a fresh abstract version of an image that had become a cliché.*
Top: courtesy of the Phyllis Kind Gallery, New York. Bottom: Private collection, Dallas, Texas. Courtesy of the George Adams Gallery, New York.

words had to be read as the Founders had understood them. But liberals fought back by challenging the whole concept of "original intent." Lawrence Tribe, a law professor at Harvard University, argued that the words of the Bill of Rights were not frozen in time at the moment Madison penned them. The Constitution was a living document, designed by the Founders to preserve rights even as American society changed. When new issues and problems arose in American life—changing assumptions about abortion, for example—the Bill of Rights provided guidance with amendments that protected the individual's control over his or her private life. It didn't matter that Madison and his colleagues hadn't written specific amendments protecting abortion, contraception, or gay rights; the broad guarantees they had provided for individual freedom were enough.

Besides, Tribe asked, was it really so easy to tell what the "original intent" of the framers and ratifiers was, as Bork claimed? What, for example, had Madison meant in the Sixth Amendment by the right of the accused to a "speedy" trial? Was that a right to a trial after two days' imprisonment? two months'? two years'? In reality, the history of the Supreme Court was a story of shifting and often dramatically contradictory understandings of what the framers had intended. At different times, judges had interpreted Madison's amendments to protect the rights of slaveowners or ex-slaves, big business or labor unions, conservatives or liberals. Justices would continue to use the Constitution to defend and expand freedoms, and rightly so. The framers had deliberately written a document for the future, a document that was broad enough to provide rules for preserving the people's liberties in situations that James Madison and his colleagues never dreamed of. "We do not attempt to offer the last word on the Constitution's meaning," Tribe maintained; "when a last word is possible the Constitution will have lost its relevance to an ever-changing society."

At the end of a bitter campaign in which conservatives lined up to applaud Bork and liberals rallied to assail him, the Democratic Senate voted to defeat his confirmation as Supreme Court justice. Yet the battle over original intent was not over. Today, liberal and conservative legal experts and politicians con-

The nomination of Robert Bork to the Supreme Court arrayed liberals against conservatives and raised questions about the Founders' intentions in ratifying the Constitution. Here, Bork supporters led by Congressman Jack Kemp rally in front of the Reagan White House.
Courtesy of AP/Wide World Photos.

tinue to argue over what the Founders intended when they drafted a Constitution for a new and revolutionary nation.

☞ *Judging the Past*

In the 1990s Americans continue to bring the Founders back to life. As has been the case for two centuries, they often disagree—sometimes angrily—about how we should confront the meaning of the Revolution and the men and women who made it.

"You are all going to watch!" shouted a weeping Christy Coleman, facing a crowd of two thousand people from the steps of Wetherburn's Tavern in

The 1994 reenactment of a slave auction at Colonial Williamsburg sparked heated debate about how to remember a painful past. Courtesy of the Colonial Williamsburg Foundation.

Williamsburg, Virginia, on October 10, 1994. "I want you to judge with honest hearts and open minds." The occasion was the first reenactment of a slave auction at the "living history" museum of Colonial Williamsburg. For decades, the museum had focused on the lives of Thomas Jefferson, Patrick Henry, George Washington, and other white Virginians while ignoring the slaves these men had bought and owned. As part of the effort to present a more accurate picture of Williamsburg's past, four African-American actors, including Coleman, were about to mount the auction block to re-create a slave sale in 1773.

But amidst the crowd of sightseers and other actors portraying white bidders, black demonstrators sang "We Shall Overcome" and held signs reading

"SAY NO TO RACIST SHOWS." "As far as we have come, to go back to this, for entertainment, is despicable and disgusting," commented Dr. Milton A. Reid, one of the protesters. "This is the kind of anguish we need not display."

As tourists took snapshots and network television crews videotaped the scene, a white actor paid seventy pounds sterling for Billy, a carpenter whose wooden box of tools were thrown in as an extra bonus. Sukie, a laundress, was bought by her husband, a free black man. But the purchaser of Daniel, a house slave dressed in green velvet breeches and a black three-cornered hat, refused to buy Daniel's pregnant wife, Lucy, despite her tearful pleas. As happened in the America of the Founding Fathers, man and wife, sold to two different owners, were separated forever.

Participants and spectators remained divided in their reactions to the auction. Eran Owens, who played Daniel, confessed to mixed emotions on the auction block: "I felt proud. I felt angry. I felt extreme sadness." While some came away persuaded that the reenactment had honored rather than exploited their ancestors, others weren't so sure. "If you want to show slavery, don't do it with some watered-down version where people clap at the end," complained Jelani Roper, an African-American senior at Thomas Jefferson's alma mater, the College of William and Mary. But Rosalind Smith was glad she had brought her nine-year-old daughter Christina: "I wanted her to see it so she would really know that it happened and that there's nothing to be ashamed of." A drained Robert Watson, Jr., the actor who portrayed Billy the carpenter, expressed a feeling shared by all: "Living history is hard on a lot of people."

As hard as that history may be, it remains alive because who we are and who we will be are rooted in who we have been. The world of the Founders—a world of freedom and slavery, of high ideals and imperfect human beings—has a hold on us, for their America gave birth to our America. The complexities and contradictions of their time, and the ever-shifting vantage points of those who look back to it, will continue to spark debates, disagreements, and arguments. Tomorrow the answers to our questions about the Founders will change again as Americans persist in understanding the past by looking to the present, and defining themselves in the present by drawing on the past.

Notes with Selected Bibliography

☞ *In most cases, direct quotations that appear in this book follow the spelling, capitalization, and punctuation of the original texts. In a few places, however, archaic or incorrect spellings and punctuation have been modernized or corrected to avoid distracting the reader.*

Dozens of primary and secondary sources were consulted in the course of researching this book. The following bibliographical notes do not constitute a comprehensive list of all relevant sources. Rather, they are intended to guide students, teachers, and general readers to works I found to be especially noteworthy, to point out books that have played a part in shaping American thought about the Founders, and to highlight the sources of particularly important or interesting quotations.

Four scholarly works were especially useful in raising and framing questions about the shifting meanings of the Founders and their Revolution: two books by Michael Kammen, *A Season of Youth: The American Revolution and the Historical Imagination* (New York: Oxford University Press, 1978) and *Mystic Chords of Memory: The Transformation of Tradition in American Culture* (New York: Knopf, 1991); Wesley Frank Craven, *The Legend of the Founding Fathers* (Ithaca: Cornell University Press, 1956); and Philip S. Foner, editor, *We, The Other People: Alternative Declarations of Independence by Labor Groups, Farmers, Woman's Rights Advocates, Socialists, and Blacks, 1829–1975* (Urbana: University of Illinois Press, 1976). As a guide to the broader historical setting of many of the disagreements and conflicts discussed throughout this book, the American Social History Project's *Who*

Built America? (New York: Pantheon Books, 1989 and 1992; Volume One covers 1607 to 1877 and Volume Two, 1877 to 1991) offers a refreshing, provocative textbook account of American history as experienced by the nation's working people, accompanied by many striking pictures. A CD-ROM version of part of Volume Two called *Who Built America? From the Centennial Celebration of 1876 to the Great War of 1914* is available from the Voyager Company.

☞ *Frankin, Washington, and the Rod*

For Adams on Franklin and Washington (8), see John Adams to Benjamin Rush, April 4, 1790, courtesy the Adams Papers. Benjamin Franklin's *Autobiography* — available in various reprint editions — is the starting point for any study of his life and the source of most of the Franklin quotations used here. The edition of the *Autobiography* in the Bedford Books in American History series (Boston: St. Martin's Press, 1993) includes an insightful introduction by Louis P. Masur that discusses Franklin's role-playing. A useful brief overview of his life is Alice J. Hall's "Benjamin Franklin, Philosopher of Dissent," *National Geographic*, Vol. 148, No. 1., July 1975, 92–123. Nian-Sheng Huang, *Benjamin Franklin in American Thought and Culture, 1790–1990* (Philadelphia: American Philosophical Society, 1994) is a fascinating account of his changing image and reputation over two centuries.

For Franklin in France, and remarks by French commentators (9), see Durand Echeverria, *Mirage in the West: A History of the French Image of American Society to 1815* (Princeton: Princeton University Press, 1957), especially pages 17–19, 22–31, 45–62, 69, 75, 109, 140, 160, 170–71. The English propaganda against him (15) is in Echeverria, 62. For Franklin and "*a rising* people" (17), see Franklin's *Autobiography* (page 82 in the Bedford Books edition).

James Thomas Flexner's *Washington: The Indispensable Man* (Boston: Little, Brown & Company, 1969) is an absorbing and thorough biography. Barry Schwartz, *George Washington: The Making of an American Symbol* (New York: Free Press, 1987) and Garry Wills, *Cincinnatus: George Washington and the Enlightenment* (Garden City, N.Y.: Doubleday & Company, Inc., 1984) both illuminate Washington's role as symbol in American culture. Mason L. Weems, *The Life of Washington* (Cambridge: Harvard University Press, 1962) includes a helpful introduction by Marcus Cunliffe that discusses Weems's career.

For Washington as "benevolent god" (17), see Schwartz, 23. The "*Landes Vater*" description (17) is in James Truslow Adams, editor in chief, *Dictionary of American History* (New York: Charles Scribner's Sons, 1940), 254. For Jefferson (18) and Hamilton (18) on Washington's temperament, see Flexner, 46–47, and Schwartz, 187. Benjamin Rush's enthusiastic comment (18) is in Schwartz, 19. Washington's response to Congress upon his appointment as general (20) is quoted in Flexner, 60–61. George III's alleged comment (20) is recounted in Wills, 13. For Ezra Stiles on Washington (22), and opposition to treating him like a god (22), see Schwartz, 41, 42–43. Washington feeling like a culprit is in Flexner, 214; Washington walking on untrodden ground, Flexner, 220. The president's remark to Humphreys is in Flexner, 227. The hostile newspaper jibes (24) and (25) are quoted in Schwartz, 54, 71; Washington's reaction (25) is discussed in Flexner, 288, 295, 346. Washington on the last day of his term, see Flexner, 347. The cherry-tree story (27) can be found in Weems, 12.

Noble E. Cunningham, Jr.'s *In Pursuit of Reason: The Life of Thomas Jefferson* (Baton Rouge: Louisiana State University Press, 1987) is a lucid and relatively concise biography. Merrill D. Peterson, editor, *The Portable Thomas Jefferson* (New York: Viking Press, 1975), is an indispensable collection of Jefferson's writings, including many fascinating private letters. Natalie S. Bober's *Thomas Jefferson: Man on a Mountain* (New York: Macmillan Publishing Company, 1988) is a comprehensive biography for young adults. Dumas Malone's six-volume *Jefferson and His Time* (Boston: Little, Brown and Company, 1948–1981) is studded with insights into Jefferson's personality and role-playing. Volume Four, *Jefferson the President: First Term, 1801–1805,* has discussions of Jefferson's dinner table protocol (367–92) and Callender's attacks (206–23). Merrill D. Peterson's classic *The Jefferson Image in the American Mind* (London: Oxford University Press, 1960) traces the Virginian's changing role as national symbol.

For Jefferson's writing desk (27), see Michael Kammen, *Mystic Chords of Memory: The Transformation of Tradition in American Culture* (New York: Knopf, 1991), 194–95. For John Adams on Jefferson in Congress (28), see "Historical Note by the Authors," Stone and Edwards, *1776: A Musical Play* (New York: Viking Press, 1970), 156. For Jefferson's confidence in the people (30), see Peterson, ed., *The Portable Thomas Jefferson,* 558; his discussion of music (30) is also in that anthology, 359. The description of Jefferson's appearance before a 1790 Senate committee (30) is quoted in Cunningham, 139. For "lions, tygers, hyaenas" (31), see Peterson, ed., *The Portable Thomas Jefferson,* 434. For the president's "diary" (32), see Francis Coleman Rosenberger, editor, *Jefferson Reader* (New York: E. P. Dutton & Co., Inc., 1953), 103–5. For Jefferson's glance (32), "King Thomas" (32), and charges of atheism (32), see Dumas Malone, *Jefferson the President: First Term, 1801–1805,* 190, 197, 373–74. For Callender on Sally Hemings (33), Jefferson on Callender (33–34), and the "Monticellian Sally" song (33–34), see Fawn Brodie, *Thomas Jefferson: An Intimate History* (New York: W. W. Norton & Co., 1974), 349, 348, 360, 354. For Jefferson and Sally Hemings, see also notes for chapter nine, "The Spirit of '76?"

For Jefferson on newspapers (34), see Peterson, ed., *The Portable Thomas Jefferson,* 505. Chastellux (34) is quoted in Cunningham, 79–80. Jefferson's letter on all eyes opening to the rights of man (34–35) is also in Peterson, ed., *The Portable Thomas Jefferson,* 584–85. Jefferson's epitaph can be found in Cunningham, 349.

☞ *Did Anybody Ever See Washington Naked?*

For John Adams's comment on Jefferson surviving him (36), see Merrill D. Peterson, *The Jefferson Image in the American Mind* (London: Oxford University Press, 1960), 3–8. The question put to New York's budding Ben Franklins (37) is reprinted in Paul A. Gilje and Howard B. Rock, editors, *Keepers of the Revolution: New Yorkers at Work in the Early Republic* (Ithaca: Cornell University Press, 1992), 53. For the 1856 New York lecture on George Washington (40), see Barry Schwartz, *George Washington: The Making of an American Symbol* (New York: Free Press, 1987), 195. Schwartz, 1, also covers criticism of the "man worship" of Washington (42). For Nathaniel Hawthorne's comment (42), see Garry Wills, *Cincinnatus: George Washington and the Enlightenment* (Garden City: Doubleday & Company, Inc., 1984), 68.

For Lowell mill workers on "Patriotic Ancestors" (45), see Thomas Dublin, "Women, Work and Protest in the Early Lowell Mills: 'The Oppressing Hand of Avarice Would Enslave Us,' " in Milton Cantor, editor, *American Workingclass Culture: Explorations in American Labor and Social History* (Westport: Greenwood Press, 1979), 177. For the Founding Fathers as strikers (46), see Michael Kammen, *A Season of Youth: The American Revolution and the Historical Imagination* (New York: Oxford University Press, 1978), 289, note 30.

The starting point for understanding Thomas Paine's influence in the American Revolution is his *Common Sense,* reprinted in numerous modern editions; I used the version in Harry Hayden Clark, editor, *Thomas Paine* (New York: Hill and Wang, Inc., 1944). Eric Foner's *Tom Paine and Revolutionary America* (London: Oxford University Press, 1976) is an excellent introduction to Paine's world and his place in it. Paine's choice of one honest man over crowned ruffians (47) is in Clark, ed., "Common Sense," 18. His comments on the age of revolutions (47) and on the Bible and science (47–48) can be found in Foner, 216 and 246–47, respectively. For Paine and his landlady's linen (50), see William Cobbett's *Porcupine's Gazette & United States Daily Advertiser* (Philadelphia), March 7, 1797. For celebrations of *The Age of Reason* (51), and Paine's use of plain language (51), see Foner, 266 and 83, respectively.

☞ *This Fourth of July Is* Yours, *Not* Mine

Paine's question on slavery (52) is quoted in Eric Foner, *Tom Paine and Revolutionary America* (London: Oxford University Press, 1976), 73. For Washington's views and actions regarding slavery (53), see James Thomas Flexner, *Washington: The Indispensable Man* (Boston: Little, Brown & Company, 1969), 385–94.

Jefferson's complex feelings about slavery and African-Americans (53–55) are best approached through his *Notes on the State of Virginia,* especially Queries XIV and XVIII; I used the W. W. Norton & Company edition (New York, 1954), edited by William Peden. Selected letters in Merrill D. Peterson, editor, *The Portable Thomas Jefferson* (New York: Viking Press, 1975), especially those to Benjamin Banneker, 454–55, Edward Coles, 544–47, and John Holmes, 567–69, also shed light on his views. John Chester Miller, *The Wolf by the Ears: Thomas Jefferson and Slavery* (Charlottesville: University Press of Virginia, 1991) and William W. Freehling, "The Founding Fathers and Slavery," in Allen Weinstein and Frank Otto Gatell, editors, *American Negro Slavery: A Modern Reader,* second edition (New York: Oxford University Press, 1973), 207–23, both offer scholarly overviews.

For slavery as tyranny (53), see Peden, ed., 162. For Jefferson's comment that "these people are to be free" (53), see Peden, ed., 287. For his assertion about "degree of talent" and rights (54), see Peterson, ed., 517.

For Garrison's denunciation of the Constitution (56), see Russel B. Nye, *William Lloyd Garrison and the Humanitarian Reformers* (Boston: Little, Brown and Company, 1955), 143. Susan B. Anthony's lament (56) can be found in Ellen Carol DuBois, editor, *Elizabeth Cady Stanton / Susan B. Anthony: Correspondence, Writings, Speeches* (New York: Schocken Books, 1981), 72. For James T. Woodbury's anecdote (56), see William C. Nell, *The Colored Patriots of the American Revolution* (1855; reprint, New York: Arno Press and the *New York Times,* 1968), 221.

Nell's fight for recognition of Attucks and other black revolutionaries (56–60) is recounted in his book, cited above. For Nell's life, see Rayford W. Logan and Michael R. Winston, editors, *Dictionary of American Negro Biography* (New York: W. W. Norton & Company, 1982), 472–73, and Dumas Malone, editor, *Dictionary of American Biography,* Volume VII (New York: Charles Scribner's Sons, 1934), 413. For African-Americans in the Revolution, see also Sidney Kaplan, *The Black Presence in the Era of the American Revolution* (Washington: National Portrait Gallery / New York Graphic Society Ltd., 1973), and for younger readers, Burke Davis, *Black Heroes of the American Revolution* (San Diego: Harcourt Brace Jovanovich, 1976). For Douglass on the Fourth of July (59), see Philip S. Foner, *The Life and Writings of Frederick Douglass*, Volume II, *Pre-Civil War Decade, 1850–1860* (New York: International Publishers, 1950), 189. For Nell on Burns and Attucks (60) and his expectancy regarding "Patriots of the Second Revolution" (60), see his book, 18 and 380, respectively.

Feminist Angelina Grimke's comment (61) is quoted by Gerda Lerner, *The Grimke Sisters from South Carolina: Pioneers for Women's Rights and Abolition* (New York: Schocken Books, 1971), 353. For Benjamin and Deborah Franklin (62), see Stanton in DuBois, ed., 137, and Louis P. Masur's introduction to *The Autobiography of Benjamin Franklin* (New York: St. Martin's Press, 1993), 8, 10. For the Seneca Falls "Declaration of Sentiments and Resolutions" (62), see Philip S. Foner, editor, *We, The Other People: Alternative Declarations of Independence by Labor Groups, Farmers, Woman's Rights Advocates, Socialists, and Blacks, 1829–1975* (Urbana: University of Illinois Press, 1976), 77–83.

Elizabeth Ellet's *The Women of the American Revolution* (63), first published in 1848, went through numerous editions. I consulted the fourth edition (1850; reprint, New York, Haskell House Publishers, Ltd., 1969). For biographies of Ellet, Mercy Otis Warren, and Deborah Sampson, see Edward T. James, editor, *Notable American Women 1607–1950: A Biographical Dictionary*, 3 volumes (Cambridge: Harvard University Press, 1971). For Sampson, see also *Publications of the Sharon Historical Society of Sharon, Massachusetts*, No. 2, April 1905, especially 5–11, and Ellet, 126. For Hannah Winthrop's assertion (68), see Ellet, 113.

William Alfred Bryan, *George Washington in American Literature: 1775–1865* (New York: Cornell University Press, 1952), 75, discusses John C. Calhoun's assertion (68). Georgia Senator Robert Toombs's remark on Jefferson (69) is in Peterson, *The Jefferson Image in the American Mind* (London: Oxford University Press, 1960), 194–95.

Eric Foner's *Free Soil, Free Labor, Free Men: The Ideology of the Republican Party Before the Civil War* (London: Oxford University Press, 1970) provides a penetrating scholarly discussion of how Lincoln and other Republicans interpreted the Revolution and its key documents (69–72). For Lincoln on Weems, see Roy Basler, editor, *The Collected Works of Abraham Lincoln*, Volume IV (New Brunswick: Rutgers University Press, 1953), 235–36. For Lincoln on the antislavery views and actions of the Founders (69), see Basler, ed., Volume III, 531–32, 535. For Lincoln on the Declaration of Independence and Jefferson (69–70), see Don E. Fehrenbacher, editor, *Abraham Lincoln: A Documentary Portrait Through His Speeches and Writings* (Stanford: Stanford University Press, 1964), 90–91, 120. See also Peterson, *Jefferson Image*, 221.

The comparison between 1861 and 1776 (70) is quoted in Michael Kammen, *A Season of Youth: The American Revolution and the Historical Imagination* (New York: Oxford University Press, 1978), 57. Emory M. Thomas, *The Confederate Nation: 1861–1865* (New York: Harper & Row, 1979), 104, 221–24; Peterson, *Jefferson Image*, 213–14; and Schwartz, *George Washington: The Making of an American Symbol*, 195, cover the ways Southerners remembered the Revolution during the Civil War (70). For "The Song of Marion's Men" (73), see William Cullen Bryant, *Poems* (Philadelphia: Carey and Hart, 1849), 223–25; see also Kammen, 119.

Richie Havens sings "Give Us a Flag" (73), written by an unknown soldier of the Massachusetts 54th Regiment, on the album *Songs of the Civil War* (New York: Sony Music Entertainment Inc., 1991). Francis Parkman's assertion (75) is quoted in Kammen, *A Season of Youth*, 35. For Washington welcoming Lincoln to heaven (75), see Schwartz, 195–97.

☞ *The Disease of Democracy*

Henry D. Northrop's insistence on Indian extinction (80) is in his *Indian Horrors or, Massacres by the Red Men* (Philadelphia: Metropolitan Publishing Co., 1891), 580. For Jane McCrea (81–82), see Bart McDowell, *The Revolutionary War: America's Fight for Freedom* (Washington, D.C.: National Geographic Society, 1967), 112; for the poem about McCrea (82), see Kenneth Silverman, *A Cultural History of the American Revolution* (New York: Thomas Y. Crowell Company, 1976), 330.

Benjamin Franklin's comment on the Iroquois (82) can be found in Carl Van Doren, *Benjamin Franklin* (New York: Viking Press, 1938), 209. For Jefferson on Indians (82–83), see his *Notes on the State of Virginia*, edited by William Peden (New York: W. W. Norton & Company, 1954), 58–63.

Peter C. Mancall, *Valley of Opportunity: Economic Culture along the Upper Susquehanna, 1700–1800* (Ithaca: Cornell University Press, 1991), 135–42, offers a vivid and scholarly account of warfare between American troops and the Iroquois (83); he quotes Washington (83), 139, and Tioguanda (83), 151–52.

For Franklin on white injustice (83), see Claude-Anne Lopez and Eugenia W. Herbert, *The Private Franklin: The Man and His Family* (New York: W. W. Norton & Company, 1975), 176. Helen Jackson, *A Century of Dishonor: A Sketch of the United States Government's Dealings with Some of the Indian Tribes* is available in a reprint edition (New York: Indian Head Books, 1993). For Jackson's remark on robbery and cruelty (83), see 27. For Washington's assurance to tribes (83), see 274. For Washington's negotiators (83–84), 44, and the Delaware chief (84), 42. For the Cherokees (84–85), see 271–74.

Robert C. Winthrop (85) is quoted in Michael Kammen, *A Season of Youth: The American Revolution and the Historical Imagination* (New York: Oxford University Press, 1978), 60–61. For the Boston Massacre monument (85), see Wesley Frank Craven, *The Legend of the Founding Fathers* (Ithaca: Cornell University Press, 1956), 171–72. For the historian John Bach McMaster's blast at Paine (85–86), see his *A History of the People of the United States from the Revolution to the Civil War* (New York: D. Appleton and Company, 1883), Volume I, 150–51. Interpretations of the Founders by late-nineteenth-century businessmen and conservatives (86) are analyzed by Craven, 147–48, and Kammen, 61–64.

For Hamilton's life and career (86–90), see Noemie Emery, *Alexander Hamilton: An Intimate Portrait* (New York: G. P. Putnam's Sons, 1982). On Hamilton's being loved and hated (86), see Henry Cabot Lodge, *Alexander Hamilton* (Boston: Houghton, Mifflin & Co., 1883), 278. For Hamilton on the need for "a firm union" (86), see Richard B. Morris, editor, *Alexander Hamilton and the Founding of the Nation* (New York: Dial Press, 1957), 137. His remark on the importance of manufactures (87) is in Emery, 144. For a "turbulent and changing" people (87), see Cecilia Kenyon's article "Alexander Hamilton: Rousseau of the Right," reprinted in Jacob E. Cooke, editor, *Alexander Hamilton: A Profile* (New York: Hill and Wang, 1967), 168. For the people as "ungovernable mob" (87), see Morris, ed., 136, and for the "disease" of "democracy" (89), see Lodge, 269. Criticisms of Hamilton (89) are reprinted in Lance Banning, *The Jeffersonian Persuasion: Evolution of a Party Ideology* (Ithaca: Cornell University Press, 1978), 168, 183, 242. Hamilton's accomplishments are praised (90) by Lodge, 279, 282, 283.

Mary E. Lease (90) is quoted in *Who Built America?* Volume Two, 147. For Jefferson on "those who labour in the earth" (92), see his *Notes on the State of Virginia*, 164–65. For his comment on cities (92), see Merrill D. Peterson, editor, *The Portable Thomas Jefferson* (New York: Viking Press, 1975), 432.

For "Cyclone" Davis (92–93), see George Brown Tindall, editor, *A Populist Reader: Selections from the Works of American Populist Leaders* (New York: Harper & Row, 1966), 203–4, 226. For William Jennings Bryan on Jefferson (95), see Paolo E. Coletta, *William Jennings Bryan* (Lincoln: University of Nebraska Press, 1964), Volume I, 182. For Bryan on grass growing "in the streets of every city" (95), see Charles Morrow Wilson, *The Commoner: William Jennings Bryan* (Garden City, N.Y.: Doubleday & Company, 1970), 451. The denunciation of the typical Populist "fanatic" (95) is from William Allen White's essay, "What's the Matter with Kansas?", reprinted in Tindall, ed., 197.

☞ One Hundred Percent Americans

For the dedication of the Statue of Liberty (97–98), see Rodman Gilder, *Statue of Liberty Enlightening the World* (New York: New York Trust Company, 1943), 31–36, and Margo Nash, *Statue of Liberty: Keeper of Dreams* (Glendale, NY: Berry Enterprises, Inc., 1983), 22. For Emma Lazarus's poem "The New Colossus" (98), see Gilder, 1.

For the reaction of the Daughters and Sons of the American Revolution and other hereditary societies to immigration (99–100), see Wesley Frank Craven, *The Legend of the Founding Fathers* (Ithaca: Cornell University Press, 1956) 158–65; Wallace Evan Davies, *Patriotism on Parade: The Story of Veterans' and Hereditary Organizations in America, 1783–1900* (Cambridge: Harvard University Press, 1955), 293–99; and John Higham, *Strangers in the Land: Patterns of American Nativism 1860–1925* (New York: Atheneum, 1963), 236–37. The S.A.R.'s immigrant education drive is discussed in Edward George Hartmann, *The Movement to Americanize the Immigrant* (New York: Columbia University Press, 1948), 32–36.

For Charles A. DeCourcey's comment, "We were foreign . . ." (102), see Craven, 168. Michael J. O'Brien's remarks (102–3) can be found in his *Irish Firsts in American History* (Chicago: American Irish Historical Society, 1917), 13–14. For Polish-American celebration of Kosciuszko (105), see Joseph A. Wytrwal, *Behold! The Polish-Americans* (Detroit: Endurance Press, 1977), 277–79, 334. Samuel Rezneck, *Unrecognized Patriots: The Jews in the American Revolution* (Westport, CT: Greenwood Press, 1975), 228–35, 277, covers Jewish-American commemorations of the Revolution and Haym Salomon (106–7). For a reprint of a portion of Washington's letter to the Newport congregation (107), see Nathan Ausubel, *Pictorial History of the Jewish People* (New York: Crown Publishers, Inc., 1953), 274.

For Albert Bernhardt Faust's comment on "families of German descent" (108), see his *The German Element in the United States* (Boston: Houghton Mifflin Company, 1909), Volume I, 336–37. Baron von Steuben's life is outlined in Dumas Malone, editor, *Dictionary of American Biography*, Volume IX (New York: Charles Scribner's Sons, 1935, 1936), 601–4. For the Steuben statue and Taft's speech (109), see Rudolf Cronau, *The Army of the American Revolution and its Organizer* (New York: privately published, 1923), 136–37.

On Viereck (109) and Skaggs (109–11) see Richard O'Connor, *The German-Americans: An Informal History* (Boston: Little, Brown and Company, 1968), 385, 392. For Viereck's assertion that "Washington fought the same enemy" (109), see *The Fatherland: A Weekly*, Vol. 1, No. 21, December 30, 1914, 11.

William H. Skaggs, *German Conspiracies in America* (London: T. Fisher Unwin Ltd., 1915), 11–12, 15–16, 18, 32, contains his assertions about the American Revolution (111). For one hundred percent Americanism and the plight of German-Americans during World War I (112–13), see Higham, 195–212, and David M. Kennedy, *Over Here: The First World War and American Society* (New York: Oxford University Press, 1980), 66–69. Wilson's "poison of disloyalty" speech (112) is quoted in Higham, 200. For "The Spirit of '76" (113), see Michael Kammen, *A Season of Youth: The American Revolution and the Historical Imagination* (New York: Oxford University Press, 1978) 172–73, and Bessie Louise Pierce, *Public Opinion and the Teaching of History in the United States* (1926; reprint, New York: Da Capo Press, 1970), 245. For the lynching of Robert Prager (113), see Kennedy, 68.

For the Steuben Society (113–14), see O'Connor, 431, and Cronau, 148–49. For an overview of the Ku Klux Klan and immigration restriction in the twenties, see Higham, 264–330. For the assertion that Washington would be a Klansman (114), see David M. Chalmers, *Hooded Americanism: The History of the Ku Klux Klan* (Durham: Duke University Press, 1987), 232.

☞ *A Slobbery Mass of Flubdub*

For Lawrence's quotes on Franklin (116), originally published in his "Studies in Classic American Literature" (1923), see the excerpts reprinted in J. A. Leo Lemay and P. M. Zall, editors, *Benjamin Franklin's Autobiography* (New York: W. W. Norton & Company, 1986) 289–99. See also Nian-Sheng Huang, *Benjamin Franklin in American Thought and Culture, 1790–1990* (Philadelphia: American Philosophical Society, 1994), 165–67. Charles A. Beard's *An Economic Interpretation of the Constitution of the United States*, originally published in 1913, has been reissued in a number of editions, including one by the Free Press (New York, 1986). Richard Hofstadter, *The Progressive Historians: Turner, Beard, Parrington* (New York: Vintage Books, 1970), 207–45, provides an illuminating overview of Beard's career and thought. For the Marion *Star* headline blasting Beard (118–19), see Hofstadter, 212.

For debunking in the twenties (120), see Michael Kammen, *A Season of Youth: The American Revolution and the Historical Imagination* (New York: Oxford University Press, 1978), 34, 69, 229, 260, and Wesley Frank Craven, *The Legend of the Founding Fathers* (Ithaca: Cornell University Press, 1956), 188–97. Williams's assessments of Burr and his peers (122–23) can be found in his *In the American Grain* (Norfolk, CT: New Directions, 1925), 192–96, 204. See W. E. Woodward, *George Washington: The Image and the Man* (New York: Boni & Liveright, 1926), for the following quotes: Washington as "a godlike character" (123–24), Preface, n.p.; the cherry-tree story (124), 16; Washington's education (125), 26; Washington and religion (125), 142; his not shaking hands (125), 437–38; his selling Tom (125), 165; Martha Custis (125), 95; his intellect (125), 429; Washington not being the Father of His Country (127), 201.

For Hughes on Washington as a "spotless saint" (127), see "Rupert Hughes Arouses Ire of Patriots by Attacking the Morals of Washington," *New York Times*, January 14, 1926, 1:6. On his love for "liquor of all kinds" (127), see Rupert Hughes, *George Washington: The Human Being & the Hero, 1732–1762* (New York: William Morrow & Company, 1926), 453. For William Lanier Washington's comment (127), see "Washington's Name Defended in Service," *New York Times*, February 22, 1926, 19:1. For the Federation of Women's Clubs (127), see "Women of Wisconsin Resent Talk of Washington Drinking," *New York Times*, October 14, 1926, 14:2. For Hughes's New York lecture (127), see "Rupert Hughes Rebuked by Woman," *New York Times*, January 16, 1926, 2:8. For S. Edward Young's comment (127–128), see "Washington 'Slurs' Branded As 'Cheap,' " *New York Times,* January 18, 1926, 24:5. For the American Legion, see Craven, 185. For Coolidge's remark (128), see " 'The Monument Is Still There,' Coolidge Says of Washington," *New York Times,* January 16, 1926, 1:2. For Washington not being "a man of first-rate ability" (128), see Woodward, 454. For "the *business mind*" (128), see Woodward, 81.

For Hughes on suppressing Washington's "outbursts" (128–129), see "Paints Washington As Great But Human," *New York Times,* November 21, 1927, 10:1. John Thornton Washington is quoted in "Admits Washington Drank, Smoked, Danced" (129), *New York Times,* January 15, 1926, 14:7. For the "schoolboy of 1926" (129), see Simeon Strunsky, "About Books, *More or Less:* Cracks in the Plaster," *New York Times,* October 31, 1926, III, 4:1.

☞ *Like the Dark Days of Valley Forge*

For "every man, woman, and child" (130), see United States George Washington Bicentennial Commission, *Papers for Programs* (Washington: 1932), n.p. Crawford's statement (132) can be found in *Orations and Essays of the George Washington Bicentennial Nation-Wide Oratorical, Essay, and Declamatory Contests in Schools and Colleges* (Washington: 1932), 7.

Russell Freedman's *Franklin Delano Roosevelt* (New York: Clarion Books, 1990) is an excellent and lively biography for young-adult readers. For Roosevelt and Monticello (134), see Merrill D. Peterson, *The Jefferson Image in the American Mind* (London: Oxford University Press, 1960), 360. For Roosevelt on Jefferson as gentleman and commoner (134), see Franklin D. Roosevelt, *Public Papers and Addresses,* Volume Five (New York: Random House, 1936), 241. For his claim concerning the anti-Jefferson press (134), see Franklin D. Roosevelt, *Public Papers and Addresses,* Volume Seven (New York: Russell & Russell, 1938), 39. Wallace's comment (135) is quoted in Peterson, 356–57.

For Strunsky's assertion (136), see Peterson, 363. The Modesto strike (137) is discussed by Bruce Nelson, *Workers on the Waterfront: Seamen, Longshoremen, and Unionism in the 1930s* (Urbana: University of Illinois Press, 1990), 178–79. For "badges of a new independence" (137), see Nelson, 267.

Smith's speech (138) is excerpted in William E. Leuchtenburg, *F.D.R. and the New Deal, 1932–1940* (New York: Harper & Row, 1963), 177–79. For Jefferson on "a wise and frugal government" (138), see his first Inaugural Address in Merrill D. Peterson, editor, *The Portable Thomas Jefferson* (New York: Viking Press, 1975), 291. For Beck's allegation (139), see Peterson, *Jefferson Image,* 370.

F.D.R.'s "economic royalist" address (139) is reprinted in Roosevelt, *Public Papers and Addresses,* Volume Five, 231–33. For Roosevelt citing Jefferson on poverty and wealth (139), see Roosevelt, *Public Papers and Addresses,* Volume Five, 486.

Bruce Nelson, 180–81, reprints the Communist poem (140–41). For Browder's assertions about the radicalism of the Founders and "twentieth century Americanism" (141), see his *What Is Communism?* (New York: Vanguard Press, 1936), 15–20, 246, and *The People's Front* (New York: International Publishers, 1938), 235. On the Young Communist League and Paul Revere (141), see James Miller, *"Democracy Is in the Streets": From Port Huron to the Siege of Chicago* (New York: Simon and Schuster, 1987), 136. For Harrison's satire on Browder (142), see Allen Guttmann, *The Wound in the Heart: America and the Spanish Civil War* (New York: Free Press of Glencoe / Macmillan, 1962), 148–49.

For *Liberation* on Franklin, and Beard's rebuttal (142–43), see Nian-Sheng Huang, *Benjamin Franklin in American Thought and Culture, 1790–1990* (Philadelphia: American Philosophical Society, 1994), 174–80. The Bund's "Pro-American Rally" (143–44) is discussed in Sander A. Diamond, *The Nazi Movement in the United States, 1924–41* (Ithaca: Cornell University Press, 1974), 324–29, and "22,000 Nazis Hold Rally in Garden," *New York Times,* February 21, 1939, 1:1. LaGuardia's response (145) is outlined in "Mayor to Permit Big Bund Meeting," *New York Times,* February 18, 1939, 30:1. Congressman Martin (145) is quoted in "Bund Meeting Here Called Traitorous," *New York Times,* February 23, 1939, 17:6.

For F.D.R.'s December 15, 1941, radio speech (146–47), see Franklin D. Roosevelt, *Public Papers and Addresses,* 1941 Volume (New York: Harper & Brothers, 1950), 555–56. For Jefferson versus Schicklgruber (147), see Peterson, *Jefferson Image,* 379.

Roosevelt's statement on national unity (147–49) is reprinted in Franklin D. Roosevelt, *Public Papers and Addresses,* 1942 Volume (New York: Harper & Brothers, 1950), 115. For F.D.R. on Mazzei (149), see Jerre Mangione and Ben Morreale, *La Storia: Five Centuries of the Italian American Experience* (New York: HarperCollins, 1992) 12–13. Roosevelt's promise to protect the Bill of Rights (149) is quoted by Michi Weglyn, *Years of Infamy: The Untold Story of America's Concentration Camps* (New York: Morrow Quill Paperbacks, 1976), 69–70.

For Paul Revere (150), see "Paul Revere Day," *New York Times,* April 19, 1942, IV, 8:2. The Washington's Birthday fireside chat (151–53) can be found in Roosevelt, *Public Papers and Addresses,* 1942 Volume (New York: Harper & Brothers, 1950), 105–17. For the North African campaign (153), see Frank L. Kluckhohn, "Front in Tunisia Like Valley Forge," *New York Times,* February 24, 1943, 2:2. Governor Martin (153) is quoted in "Calls for Harder Work," *New York Times,* June 19, 1944, 3:6.

For the Roosevelt-Jefferson resemblance (153), see Peterson, *Jefferson Image,* 360, and Arthur Krock, "Roosevelt Adventures in Role of Architect," *New York Times,* March 15, 1942, IV, 3:1. Peterson, *Jefferson Image,* discusses the creation of the Jefferson Memorial (153), 377–78, 420–36. For F.D.R. on the politics of the memorial (153–54), see Roosevelt, *Public Papers and Addresses,* Volume Seven, 605–7. For a Jefferson statue "with tears" (154), see Peterson, *Jefferson Image,* 427. His last undelivered address (155) can be found in Franklin D. Roosevelt, *Public Papers and Addresses,* 1944–45 Volume (New York: Random House, 1950), 613–16.

☞ *I Call Upon You to Be Maladjusted*

For Eisenhower's comment (157), see William E. Leuchtenburg, *A Troubled Feast: American Society Since 1945,* Revised edition (Boston: Little, Brown and Company, 1979), 84. Galbraith (157) is quoted by Richard H. Pells, *The Liberal Mind in a Conservative Age: American Intellectuals in the 1940s & 1950s* (New York: Harper & Row, 1985), 165. For a useful assessment of the consensus historians (158), see Pells, 147–62.

For McCarthy's Wheeling statements (161), see Leuchtenburg, 31. For Smith's comments and her Declaration of Conscience (163–64), see David M. Oshinsky, *A Conspiracy So Immense: The World of Joe McCarthy* (New York: Free Press, 1983), 163–65. Russell (164) is quoted by William F. Buckley, Jr., and L. Brent Bozell, *McCarthy and His Enemies: The Record and Its Meaning* (Chicago: Henry Regnery Company, 1954), 310. For White's remark (164), see Jack Anderson and Ronald W. May, *McCarthy: The Man, the Senator, the "Ism"* (Boston: Beacon Press, 1952), 384.

The fictional dialogue between McCarthy and Jefferson (165) is from the record album *The Investigator* (Discuriosities/Radio Rarities, 1954). For the slanders on Jefferson and Lincoln (166), see Buckley and Bozell, 304. For McCarthy on Jefferson (167), see Edwin R. Bayley, *Joe McCarthy and the Press* (Madison: University of Wisconsin Press, 1981), 217–18.

King's plea for maladjustment (167) can be found in James Melvin Washington, editor, *A Testament of Hope: The Essential Writings and Speeches of Martin Luther King, Jr.* (San Francisco: Harper, 1991), 14–15. For the quotation from King's "I Have a Dream" speech (168), see Washington, ed., 217. Mays (168) is quoted in Andrew Michael Manis, *Southern Civil Religions in Conflict: Black and White Baptists and Civil Rights, 1947–1957* (Athens: University of Georgia Press, 1987), 36. For Abernathy (168), see Manis, 75. For King on "the poor men of 1776" (168–69), see Washington, ed., 91–92. For Talmadge's comment (169), see Manis, 80. The Klan leaflet (169) is reprinted in *The Present-Day Ku Klux Klan Movement: Report by the Committee on Un-American Activities, House of Representatives* (Washington: U.S. Government Printing Office, 1967), 370–71.

For Johnson's Civil Rights Act comments (170), see *New York Times,* July 3, 1964, 9:2. For Malcolm X on the "American nightmare" and slave ships (170), see Steve Clark, editor, *Malcolm X Talks to Young People: Speeches in the U.S., Britain, and Africa* (New York: Pathfinder Press, 1991), 11. For his comment on Jefferson, Washington, and Henry (171), see *Malcolm X on Afro-American History* (New York: Pathfinder Press, 1970), 39. On the Revolution as a white man's war, and the Fourth of July (171), see Bruce Perry, editor, *Malcolm X: The Last Speeches* (New York: Pathfinder Press, 1989), 62. On Attucks (171), see *Malcolm X on Afro-American History,* 80. For Patrick Henry (172), see Clark, ed., 18. For Cleaver's exhortation (172), see Eldridge Cleaver, *Soul on Ice* (New York: McGraw-Hill, 1968), 19.

For Attucks Day in Newark (172–73), see *New York Times,* March 25, 1968, 47:7. For Malcolm X on "a time of extremism" (174), see Clark, ed., 25. Mills's comment on boredom and restlessness (174) is quoted in Pells, 255, and his comparison of Washington's and Eisenhower's reading (175) is in C. Wright Mills, *The Power Elite* (New York: Oxford University Press, 1956), 350.

Sharon Jeffrey (175) is quoted by James Miller, *"Democracy Is in the Streets": From Port Huron to the Siege of Chicago* (New York: Simon and Schuster, 1987), 144. For Jefferson's influence on the S.D.S. (175), see Miller, 51, 78. For Honor America Day (177–79), see *New York Times,* June 14, 1970, 44:1; June 26, 1970, 16:1; and July 5, 1970, 1:1.

For the Lexington demonstration (179), see *New York Times,* July 5, 1967, 5:4; for the reenactment of Revere's ride (179), see *New York Times,* June 1, 1971, 1:3. For Veterans and Reservists to End the War in Vietnam (179), see Joseph P. Callahan, "Parades for Peace, Brotherhood . . . (and Washington) Mark Holiday Here," *New York Times,* February 23, 1967, 24:3. For the new "Boston Tea Party" (179), see *New York Times,* April 16, 1970, 44:3.

☞ *The Spirit of '76?*

For "Poor Richard's Almanack—Nixon Edition" (181), see *New York Times,* October 21, 1970, 47:1. Hickel's letter (182–83) is quoted and discussed by Max Frankel, "Hickel, in Note to Nixon, Charges Administration Is Failing Youth," *New York Times,* May 7, 1970, 1:8; "Text of the Hickel Letter," *New York Times,* May 7, 1970, 18:3; and E. W. Kenworthy, "Hickel's Advisers Tell Why He Acted," *New York Times,* May 8, 1970, 1:6.

For "the continued existence of the Presidency" (184) and the "Jefferson rule" (184), see Anthony Lewis, "Alice in Wonderland," *New York Times*, November 19, 1973, 35:1. For Nixon on "every President since George Washington" (184), Flexner's views (185), and Washington's words to Randolph (185), see Glenn Fowler, "Washington's Waiver of Privilege in Randolph Case Is Called in Conflict with Nixon Position," *New York Times*, October 31, 1973, 31:1. For Malone's comments (186), see Dumas Malone, "President Jefferson: Subpoenas and Privilege," *New York Times*, November 26, 1973, 30:5.

"A Letter to Julie" (186) appeared in the *New York Times*, September 9, 1973, Week in Review section, 18. For Lewis on Jefferson (187), see Anthony Lewis, "Happy Birthday," *New York Times*, July 5, 1973, 29:5. See Gore Vidal, *Burr* (New York: Random House, 1973), 287, for the fictional Burr on Jefferson (187).

For Sundown's and Weigel's Bicentennial remarks (189), see Israel Shenker, "Indian Clan Isn't Inclined to Celebrate Bicentennial," *New York Times*, July 3, 1976, 8:7. The West German magazine (190) is quoted by Alfred Kazin, "Every Man His Own Revolution," *New Republic*, July 3 and 10, 1976, 24; see the same article, 23, for the " 'selling' of the Bicentennial" (190). Jesse Lemisch's comments (190) are from his "Bicentennial Schlock," *New Republic*, November 6, 1976, 22–23.

For Nash's comment (192), see the preface to his "Social Change and the Growth of Prerevolutionary Urban Radicalism" in Alfred F. Young, *The American Revolution: Explorations in the History of American Radicalism* (DeKalb: Northern Illinois University Press, 1976), 4. On Nonhelema (193), see Linda K. Kerber, *Women of the Republic: Intellect & Ideology in Revolutionary America* (Chapel Hill: University of North Carolina Press, 1980), 87. For Hewes (193), see Alfred F. Young, "George Robert Twelves Hewes (1742–1840): A Boston Shoemaker and the Memory of the American Revolution," *William and Mary Quarterly*, 3rd Series, Volume 38, No. 4, October 1981, 561–623. For Scott, Brooks, and Henderson (193), see John Shy, "Hearts and Minds in the American Revolution: The Case of 'Long Bill' Scott and Peterborough, New Hampshire," 163–79, in his *A People Numerous & Armed: Reflections on the Military Struggle for American Independence* (London: Oxford University Press, 1976). For Bailyn's approach (194), see his *The Ideological Origins of the American Revolution* (Cambridge: Harvard University Press, 1967).

For Jefferson's heart and head (194), the Randolph comment (195), and society's fault (195), see Fawn M. Brodie, *Thomas Jefferson: An Intimate History* (New York: W. W. Norton & Company, Inc., 1974): 29–30, 248, and 32, respectively. For Malone's critique (195), see "Jefferson's Private Life," *New York Times*, May 18, 1974, 31:5. A more positive review of Brodie is Alfred Kazin, *New York Times Book Review*, April 7, 1974, 1. For Kazin on Jefferson and the meaning of America (195), see *New York Times Book Review*, May 12, 1974, 42.

For John Adams to Abigail Adams (196), see L. H. Butterfield, Marc Friedlaender, and Mary-Jo Kline, editors, *The Book of Abigail and John* (Cambridge: Harvard University Press, 1975), 4. Abigail Adams's assertions about freedom (196–98) and the Southern "passion for Liberty" (198) can be found in Butterfield et al., 82 and 8, respectively. For Abigail's and John's exchange on women's rights (198), see the American Social History Project, *Who Built America?* Volume One (New York: Pantheon Books, 1989), 144.

For Bork on "timeless principles" (201), see "The Advocates," *Life*, Fall Special 1991, Volume 14, Number 13, 98. For his comment on problems and issues "placed off-limits" (201), see Robert H. Bork, *The Tempting of America: The Political Seduction of the Law* (New York: Free Press, 1990), 163. For Tribe on not offering "the last word" (202), see Lawrence H. Tribe and Michael C. Dorf, *On Reading the Constitution* (Cambridge: Harvard University Press, 1991), 31.

For the Williamsburg "slave auction" (203–5), see Tamara Jones, "Living History or Undying Racism?" *Washington Post*, October 11, 1994, A1; Leef Smith, "Williamsburg Slave Auction Riles Va. NAACP," *Washington Post*, October 11, 1994, B1; "Tears and Protest at Mock Slave Sale," *New York Times*, October 11, 1994, A16:4; Alison Freehling, "Shame of a nation re-created," *Staten Island Advance*, October 11, 1994.

Index

Davis, Rennie, 178
Debunking, 120–29, *124, 126*
Declaration of Conscience, 164
Declaration of Independence, *5,* 6, 27–28, *41,*
    46, 47, 51, 85, 96, 116, 141, 149, 158,
    168, 175, 182
    contradictory interpretations of, 3–4
    declaration of women's rights modeled on,
      62, 76
    fiftieth anniversary of, 34, 36
    immigration and, 99, 100–101
    as model for other revolutions, 97
    slavery issue and, 3, 53, 55, 60, 70
Declaration of Sentiments and Resolutions, 62
De Crow, Karen, 189
Deists, 47, 50, 51
Democracy, 156, 175
    Hamilton's views on, 87–89
    Jefferson's views on, 136, 138–39
    threatened by Depression, 135–36, 140–45
    World War II and, 151
Democratic Party, 95–96, 138, 140, 149, 156,
    160, 163
Democratic-Republican Party, 23–25, 31, 32, 33,
    50, 89
Depression, Great, 130–45, 156, 157, 163
    democracy threatened by, 135–36, 140–45
    New Deal and, 135–40, 154, 155, 199
Douglass, Frederick, 59, 63, 171, 189

Economic Interpretation of the Constitution, An
    (Beard), 117–20
Eisenhower, Dwight D., 157, 169, 175
Elizabeth II, queen of England, 188
Ellet, Elizabeth, 63–64, 68, 192
Emancipation Proclamation, 73
Enlightenment, 11, 13
Equality
    slavery issue and, 3, 54–55
    for women, 62–63
Equal Rights Amendment, 198
Executive privilege, 184–86

Fairfax, Sally, 128
"Family values," 199

Farmers, 6, 78–79, 87, 118
    Populist movement and, 90–96
Farrakhan, Louis, 171
Fascism, 135, 142–45, *144,* 149
    World War II and, 146–47, 149
Fatherland, 109, *110*
Faust, Albert, 108
Federalist Papers, The (Hamilton, Madison, and
    Jay), 87
Federalist Party, 23, *24,* 25, 31–34, 50, 89, 93,
    158–60
Federation of Women's Clubs, 127
Feminism, feminists, 60–68, 76, 85, 117, 177,
    189, 192, 194, 198
    abolitionist movement and, 60–61
    first convention of, 61–63
    Founding Fathers as viewed by, 62
    women in Revolution celebrated by, 63–68,
      65, 66, 193, 196–98
Flexner, James Thomas, 185
Ford, Gerald, 188
Fourth of July celebrations, 37, *39,* 59, *119,* 171,
    189
France:
    Franklin esteemed in, 13–15
    revolution in, 23, 47, 50, 97
    Statue of Liberty and, 97–98
Franklin, Benjamin, *5,* 6, 7, 8–17, *14,* 37, *38,* 86,
    101, 111, 123, 181
    anti-Semitism ascribed to, 142–43
    as backwoods genius, 13–15, *16*
    diplomatic mission of, 15, 62
    Europeans' admiration for, 9, 11–15
    feminists' disdain for, 62
    Lawrence's disdain for, 116–17
    Native Americans and, 82, 83
    public image of, 9, 10–11, 15, 17
    as scientist, 11–13, *12*
    slavery issue and, 53, 56, 69
    as successful businessman, 9–10
    as symbol of what America was becoming,
      17
    temperament of, 10–11
Franklin, Deborah, 62
Franklin, James, 9

Native Americans in, 80–84, *81*, 193
poorest Americans in, 193
revisionist histories of, 192–94, 196, 198
S. A. R. and D. A. R. and, 99–100, 101
slavery issue and, 52–53
Southern states' views on, 68–73
as viewed in 1920s, 122–23
as viewed in 1950s, 160–61, *162*
Washington's command in, 17, 18, 20, 22,
    104, 105, 108–9, 125, 128, 151–53, 193
women in, 63–68, *65, 66*, 193, 196–98
World War I propaganda and, 109–12, *110*,
    113
Rickenbacker, Eddie, 112
Rights of Man, The (Paine), 47, 50
Riots, of African-Americans, 170
"Robber barons," 78
Rochambeau, Comte de, 109
Rockefeller, Nelson, 188
Rockwell, Norman, *131*
Roe v. *Wade*, 199
Roosevelt, Eleanor, 136
Roosevelt, Franklin D., 132–40, 199
    critics of, 137–39, 142, 144–45
    Jefferson revered by, 153–55, *154*, 156
    World War II and, 146–53, 155
Roosevelt, Theodore, 90, *103*
Ross, Betsy, *106*
Royal Academy of Sciences (Paris), 11
Royal Society (London), 11
Rush, Benjamin, 18
Russell, Bertrand, 164

Saint-Aubin, Augustus de, *16*
Salem, Peter, 57
Salomon, Haym, 107, 115, 144, 147, *148*
Sampson, Deborah, 66–68, 161
Saul, Peter, *200*
Savalas, Telly, 188
Scott, "Long Bill," 193, 198
Senate, 84, 202
    McCarthy hearings in, 161–67
    Watergate hearings in, 184
    see also Congress
Seneca Falls Convention (1848), 61–63

1776, 196
Shays' Rebellion (1786–87), 117
Shy, John, 193
Silver Shirts, 142–43
Sioux, 79–80
Skaggs, William H., 109–12
Slavery, slaves, 3, 30, 33–34, 52–60, *54*, 125,
    160, 161, 167, 170–71, 198
    end of, 73, 74, 75
    Founding Fathers claimed as supporters of,
        68–70
    Jefferson's views on, 53–55, 69–70, 195
    North-South disagreement on, 68–70, 76
    opposition to, 55–60; *see also* Abolitionists
    and reenactment of slave auction, *204*,
        204–5
    runaways and, 59–60
    westward spread of, 58, 68, 69, 72
    "woman question" and, 60–61
Smith, Al, 138
Smith, Kate, 178
Smith, Margaret Chase, 163, 164
Smothers Brothers, 179
Socialism, Socialists, 118, 138
Sons of the American Revolution (S.A.R.),
    99–101, *101*
Sorel, Edward, *185*
South
    Civil War and, 70–74
    farmers in, 92
    racial discrimination in, 169–70
    secession of, 70–72
    slavery in, 53, 55, 59, 68–70, 76
Southern Christian Leadership Conference
    (S. C. L. C.), 167, 170
Soviet Union, 157, 163
Spanish-American War, 105–6
Speech, freedom of, 164, 166, 201
"Spirit of '76, The," 113
Stalin, Joseph, 140, 141
Standard Oil Company, 137
Stanton, Elizabeth Cady, 60–63
State Department, 161
States rights, 70–71, 169
Statue of Liberty, 97–98, 99, 114

Steuben, Baron Friedrich Wilhelm von, 108–9,
    115, 149, 150
Steuben Society, 113–14
Stiles, Ezra, 22
Strunsky, Simeon, 136
Stuart, Gilbert, *121*
Student activism, 174–80, *176,* 192
    antiwar protests and, 175–79, *176, 180,*
       182–83
Students for a Democratic Society (S. D. S.),
    175, 178, 192
Sullivan, John, 105
Sundown, Corbett, 189
Supreme Court, 117, 169, 186, 199–202

Taft, William Howard, 109
Talmadge, Herman, 169
Thayendanegea (Joseph Brant), 80
Thomas Jefferson (Brodie), 194–95
Tiebout, Cornelius, *29*
Tioguanda, 83
Toombs, Robert, 69
Treasury Department, 87, 89, 118
Tribe, Lawrence, 202
Trumbull, John, *5*
Turgot, Anne-Robert-Jacques, 13

Valley Forge, 151–53, *152,* 189, 193
Vanderbilt, Cornelius, 78
Vanderlyn, John, *81*
Van Doren, Carl, 143
Vidal, Gore, 187–88
Viereck, George Sylvester, 109
Vietnam War, 175–79, *176, 178, 180,* 182–83,
    189–90, 192, 193
Voltaire, 13, 164
Voting rights, 168–69
    of poor, 37
    of women, 61, 63, 169

Wagner Act, 137
Wallace, Henry, 135
Walt Disney Presents, 160–61, *162*
Warren, James, 64
Warren, Mercy Otis, 64, *65,* 66, 67, 68, 196

Washington, George, 5, 6, 8, 17–27, *21, 24, 26,*
    34, 35, 37, 86, 87, *91, 94,* 100, 102,
    107, 109, *110,* 114, 117, 137, 139, 150,
    154, 166, 169, 171, 175, 177, 183,
    185–90, 198, 204
    cherry-tree legend and, 27, 124, *124,* 129
    claimed by both sides in Civil War, 72
    glorification of, *19,* 20–22, 123–24, 127–29
    honored by Nazis, *144,* 144–45
    Lincoln compared to, 75–76, *76*
    military command of, 17, 18, 20, 22, *104,*
       105, 108–9, 125, 128, 151–53, 193
    as most beloved man in America, 17
    Native Americans and, 83–84
    personality of, 17–18, 20
    physical appearance of, 18
    popular enthusiasm for, in early nineteenth
       century, 40–42
    presidency of, 22–25, 30, 31, 138
    slavery issue and, 53, *54,* 56, 68, 69, 72, 125
    as target of debunkers, 123–29, *124, 126*
    temperament of, 125, 127–29
    vilified by Democratic-Republicans, 23–25
    Weems's biography of, 25–27
Washington, John Thornton, 129
Washington, Martha Custis, 53, *102,* 125, 128
Washington, William Lanier, 127
George Washington Bicentennial (1932),
    130–32, *131, 133*
Watergate, 181–88, 190
Wayne, "Mad Anthony," 189
Weaver, James, 94
Weems, Mason, 25–27, 69, 124, *124*
Weigel, Hugh, 189
West, Benjamin, *12,* 20
White, John Blake, *74*
White, William S., 164
Whitney, Eli, 55
Wilkinson, James, 184
Williams, William Carlos, 122–23, 187
Wilson, Woodrow, 109, 113
Winthrop, Hannah, 68
Winthrop, Robert C., 85
Women, 6, 44–46, 60–68, 158, 161, 177
    discrimination against, 60–61